Assessment Manual

Placement, Diagnosis, and Prescription

Research Snapshot

REGULAR ASSESSMENT IS THE KEY TO INDIVIDUALLY APPROPRIATE INSTRUCTION

Use the *Read Well* assessment system with fidelity.

Following a review of the research on normal reading development, reading instruction, and factors related to reading failure, the National Research Council (1998) recommended ongoing assessment of word recognition and fluency as a critical component of excellent reading instruction.

"Because the ability to obtain meaning from print depends so strongly on the development of word recognition accuracy and reading fluency, both the latter should be regularly assessed in the classroom, permitting timely and effective instructional response when difficulty or delay is apparent" (Snow, Burns, & Griffin, 1998, p. 7).

Critical Foundations in Primary Reading

Marilyn Sprick, Lisa Howard, Ann Fidanque, Shelley V. Jones

Copyright 2007 (Second Edition) Sopris West Educational Services. All rights reserved.

ISBN 13-digit: 978-1-59318-513-8   ISBN 10-digit: 1-59318-513-8   131351/04-22

18 19 20 21 22 FRD 26 25 24 23 22

Table of Contents

Introduction

Placement

As children enter school with their own unique literacy histories and abilities, it is crucial to take great care in placing each child in an instructional group that allows success. During the first week of school, each child is assessed for placement in a small group using the *Read Well* Placement Inventory.

Beginning Small Group Instruction

By the second or third week of school, small group instruction begins. Daily instruction focuses on the five critical areas of early reading instruction identified by the National Reading Panel (2000): phonemic awareness, phonics, fluency, vocabulary, and comprehension. Instruction is systematic, explicit, rich in content, and mastery based.

Cycle of Assessment and Instruction

Once children are in small groups, regular end-of-unit assessments provide ongoing progress monitoring. Prescriptive teaching follows diagnosis with lesson planning and instruction tailored to the developmental needs of each group and every child. Guidelines for acceleration, early intervention, and group reviews guide a process that maximizes the progress of each child.

Every Child Deserves to *Read Well*®

SECTION 1

Placement

This section explains how to use the Placement Inventory to group students for success.

Overview

Recognizing that schools often have their own battery of extensive and required assessments, the *Read Well* Placement Inventory quickly but accurately assesses students' skills for preliminary group placement. Once small group instruction begins, group membership often changes based on each student's response to instruction.

The Placement Inventory has two parts.

Placement Inventory Part 1

Part 1 is administered to all students and assesses:

- Knowledge of capital letter names
- Knowledge of small letter sounds
- Knowledge of high-frequency words
- Knowledge of pattern words

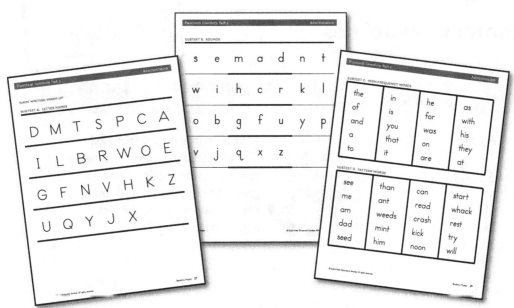

3

Placement Inventory Part 2

Part 2 is administered only to students who are able to identify 11 or more letters and sounds and read five or more words from Part 1. Part 2 consists of selected end-of-unit *Read Well 1* Decoding Assessments and Oral Reading Fluency Assessments.

Part 2 includes Decoding Assessments from Units 3, 5, 9, and 15. The assessments measure:

- Knowledge of sounds
- Knowledge of blending
- Knowledge of irregular words
- Ability to read sentences accurately and with fluency

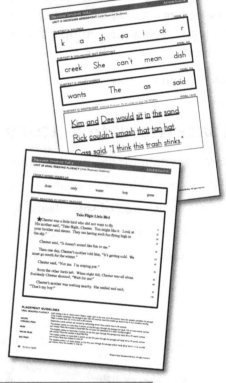

If students score Strong Passes, they continue with Oral Reading Fluency Assessments from Units 20, 23, 29, and 38.
These assessments measure:

- Knowledge of Tricky Words
- Oral reading fluency

Placement Guidelines

Children can place in many potential entry points.

ENTRY	PLACEMENT GUIDELINES
• Unit A (Intervention) • Unit 1 • Unit 4 • Unit 6 • Unit 10 • Unit 16 • Unit 21 • Unit 24 • Unit 30 • *Read Well Plus*	**Place students conservatively.** Once instruction begins, students can be moved easily from one group to the next. If in doubt, place students in the lowest appropriate group.

Once all Placement Inventories are completed, compromises can be made to accommodate group placement, but no child should ever be placed at a higher level than his or her score indicates. All children should experience success from the start of instruction.

Managing the Placement Inventory

When to Administer

The Placement Inventory should be administered to all first grade students and remedial second and third grade students during the first week of school. A quick start is strongly recommended as the loss of a week or two of instruction can make the difference in whether a high-risk child achieves grade level or not.

Who Administers

The first weeks of school are a time of newness and uncertainty for young children. Because classroom teachers are fully occupied meeting the needs of their students, assessments should be administered outside of class time or by other trained professionals. As each school varies in its opening routines and resources, some options to consider are to:

- Have an assessment team administer the Placement Inventory to individual students while the teacher continues teaching.

- Have another trained professional administer the Placement Inventory during parent–teacher conferences.

- Have a trained professional administer the Placement Inventory at the time the student registers.

If assistance is not available, classroom teachers should assess a few students each day—completing placement testing in the first two weeks of school.

Research Snapshot

A STRONG START

Juel (1988) studied the literacy development of children from first through fourth grade. In that study, Juel found a .88 correlation between how a child was reading at the end of first grade and how a child was reading at the end of fourth grade. In other words, there is a high probability that children who are poor readers at the end of first grade will remain poor readers. Few children magically catch up after a slow start.

Materials Preparation

1. Make one copy per student of the Student Placement Record, Part 1 and Part 2 Summary (page 49). This form is used to record and score students responses. Keep the Student Placement Record in each student's file or portfolio as a pretest measure.

2. Make additional copies of the Student Placement Record, Part 2 (pages 50–54). Part 2 will only be used with children who score 26 or more on Part 1. The student record forms for Part 2 can be stapled to Part 1 as needed.

3. For each person who will administer the Placement Inventory, make one copy of the Placement Inventory on pages 37–48. You may wish to laminate the administration pages or place the pages in plastic sheet protectors.

4. Obtain stopwatches. The assessments for Units 9 and higher include timings to measure students' reading fluency.

5. Place the Student Placement Records on clipboards for each person administering the Placement Inventory.

6. Set up a quiet place to administer the Placement Inventory. Students should be seated at a table.

Student Placement Record
Part 1 and Part 2 Summary

Student Placement Record Part 2

Placement Inventory Part 1

Administration Guidelines

Part 1 of the Placement Inventory is composed of a warm-up activity and four subtests: letter names, letter sounds, high-frequency words, and pattern words.

When administering the Placement Inventory:

- Assess each child individually, away from others.

- Record student responses on the Student Placement Record, Part 1. Record a "plus" for each correct response and a "minus" for each incorrect response.

- For each item, wait three seconds. If the student does not respond, struggles, or gives an incorrect response, gently tell the student the letter name, sound, or word and score the item as incorrect. Then encourage the student to copy your response.

  Say something like:

  That's /aaa/.
  Say it with me. **/aaa/**
  That's right. That letter says /aaa/.

  With this simple procedure, children view this early assessment as a learning experience, rather than a test.

- On each subtest, stop if the student makes five consecutive errors. Point to the remaining rows or columns and ask the student if he or she knows any of the letters, sounds, or words. Give credit for any correct responses.

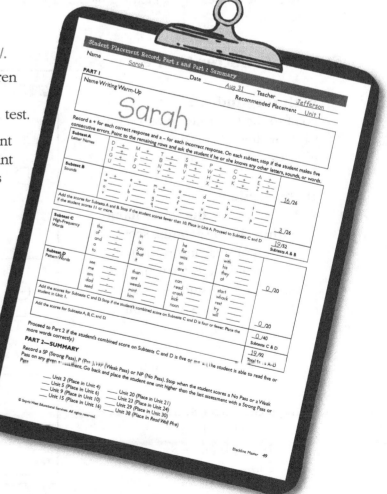

How to Administer the Subtests

Name Writing Warm-Up

Name writing provides an informal assessment of a student's literacy background.

With the student:

Point to the box at the top of the Student Placement Record and have the student write his or her name. Say something like: Can you write your name for me?

If the student:

- **Has difficulty, compliment the student on something she or he can do.** Say something like: That's great! You can write an E for "Emily."

- **Is able to write his or her first name with ease, ask the student to write his or her last name.** Say something like: Wow! You can write "Emily." Can you also write your last name?

Subtest A. Letter Names

With the student:

Point to the first letter in Subtest A. Say something like: I'd like you to point to each letter and say its name.

If the student:

- **Does not say the letter name within three seconds**, score the response as incorrect. Tell the student the letter name, then encourage the student to say the letter name. Say something like:

    That's the letter M.
    What letter is that? (M)
    That's right.

- **Says the letter sound**, say something like:

    That's the letter sound.
    Can you tell me the letter name?

If the student says the letter name with your prompt, score this as a correct response.

Reproducible Placement Inventory Part I, Warm-Up and Subtest A available on page 37.

Subtest B. Sounds

With the student:

Point to the first letter in Subtest B. Say something like:

> I'd like you to point to each letter and tell me its sound.

If the student:

- **Does not say the letter sound within three seconds**, score the response as incorrect. Tell the student the letter sound, then encourage the student to say the letter sound.

- **Says the letter name**, say something like:

  > That's the letter name. Do you know its sound?

  If the student says the letter sound with your prompt, score this as a correct response.

- **Says the letter name for a vowel** (the long vowel sound), say something like:

  > Yes, can you tell me another sound for that letter?

  Score only the short sounds (as in "ant," "in," "end," "on," and "up") as correct.

- **Says the soft sound for g (as in "giant") or for <u>c</u> (as in "circus")**, say something like:

  > Yes, can you tell me another sound for that letter?

  Score only the hard sounds (as in "gorilla" and "cat") as correct.

- **Says a quick (or stop) sound consonant with a vowel sound (/duh/, rather than /d/)**, score the response as correct, but note pronunciation. (For ease of blending, quick pronunciation of stop sounds will be taught and assessed during instruction.)

Placement Inventory Part 1   Administration

SUBTEST B. SOUNDS

s	e	m	a	d	n	t
w	i	h	c	r	k	l
o	b	g	f	u	y	p
v	j	q	x	z		

Reproducible Placement Inventory Part 1, Subtest B available on page 38.

PLACEMENT GUIDELINES

STOP Stop if the student scores 10 or fewer correct. Place the student in Unit A.

Proceed to Subtests C and D if the student scores 11 or more.

Subtest C. High-Frequency Words

With the student:
Have the student read the words. Point to the first word in Subtest C.
Say something like:

You can read letter names and sounds. I'd like to see if you can read words too.
Point to each word and tell me what you think it says.

If the student:

- **Reads a word as it is pronounced within three seconds**, score the response as correct.

- **Does not attempt a word within three seconds**, score the response as incorrect. Tell the student the word and encourage him or her to say the word.

- **Sounds out a word as it looks, but not as it is pronounced**, say:

    How do you say that word?

If the student then pronounces the word correctly, it is correct.
For example, if a student sounds out "is" as follows: /iiisss/, you would say:

    How do you say that word?

If a student says /iz/, the response is correct.

Subtest D. Pattern Words

With the student:
Have the student read the words.
Point to the first row of words in Subtest D.
Say something like:

    I'd like to see if you can read any of
    these. Point to the first word and see
    if you can tell me what it says.

PLACEMENT GUIDELINES

STOP Stop if the student's combined score on Subtests C and D is four or fewer correct. Place the student in Unit 1.

Proceed to Part 2 if the student's combined score on Subtests C and D is five or more correct.

If the student:

- **Sounds out a word correctly**, score the response as correct.

- **Struggles with the word or does not attempt a word within three seconds**, score the response as incorrect. Tell the student the word and encourage the student to say the word. Say something like:

    That's a hard word. It says "see." Tell me the word. **(see)**

SUBTEST C. HIGH-FREQUENCY WORDS

the	in	he	as	**Subtest C High-Frequency Words**
of	is	for	with	
and	you	was	his	
a	that	on	they	
to	it	are	at	

SUBTEST D. PATTERN WORDS

see	than	can	start	**Subtest D Pattern Words**
me	ant	read	whack	
am	weeds	crash	rest	
dad	mint	kick	try	
seed	him	noon	will	

Blackline Master 39

Reproducible Placement Inventory Part 1, Subtests C and D available on page 39.

Sergio's Example

Warm-Up

Sergio was able to write his first name, mixing capital letters and small letters. He was not able to write his last name.

Subtests A and B

Sergio demonstrated knowledge of 16 letter names and three sounds. He knows only three sounds—the sounds introduced in whole class instruction. Because Sergio scored more than 11 on Subtests A and B, he was given Subtests C and D.

Subtests C and D

Sergio was unable to read any of the words on Subtests C and D, so he places in Unit 1. Sergio will not be given Part 2.

Total Score

Sergio's total score was 19. If more than one group begins instruction with Unit 1, Sergio's total score will be used to place him with students who most closely match his skills at the time of testing.

Student Placement Record, Part 1 and Part 2 Summary

Name ____Sergio____   Date ____Aug 31____   Teacher ____Jefferson____

Recommended Placement ____Unit 1____

PART 1

Name Writing Warm-Up

SFrgIo

Record a + for each correct response and a – for each incorrect response. On each subtest, stop if the student makes five consecutive errors. Point to the remaining rows and ask the student if he or she knows any other letters, sounds, or words.

Subtest A — Letter Names

D +	M +	T +	S +	P +	C –	A +
I +	L –	B +	R +	W –	O +	E –
G +	F –	N +	V –	H +	K +	Z +
U –	Q –	Y –	J –	X +		**16 /26**

Subtest B — Sounds

s +	e +	m +	a ___	d ___	n ___	t ___
w ___	i ___	h ___	c ___	r ___	k ___	l ___
o ___	b ___	g ___	f ___	u ___	y ___	P ___
v ___	j ___	q ___	x ___	z ___		**3 /26**

Add the scores for Subtests A and B. Stop if the student scores fewer than 10. Place in Unit A. Proceed to Subtests C and D if the student scores 11 or more.   **19 /52** — Subtests A & B

Subtest C — High-Frequency Words

the –	in ___	he ___	as ___
of –	is ___	for ___	with ___
and –	you ___	was ___	his ___
a –	that ___	on ___	they ___
to –	it ___	are ___	at ___

0 /20

Subtest D — Pattern Words

see –	than ___	can ___	start ___
me –	ant ___	read ___	whack ___
am –	weeds ___	crash ___	rest ___
dad –	mint ___	kick ___	try ___
seed –	him ___	noon ___	will ___

0 /20

Add the scores for Subtests C and D. Stop if the student's combined score on Subtests C and D is four or fewer. Place the student in Unit 1.   **0 /40** — Subtests C & D

Add the scores for Subtests A, B, C, and D.   **19 /92** — Total Score A–D

Proceed to Part 2 if the student's combined score on Subtests C and D is five or more. (The student is able to read five or more words correctly.)

PART 2—SUMMARY

Record a SP (Strong Pass), P (Pass), WP (Weak Pass) or NP (No Pass). Stop when the student scores a No Pass or a Weak Pass on any given assessment. Go back and place the student one unit higher than the last assessment with a Strong Pass or Pass.

___ Unit 3 (Place in Unit 4)   ___ Unit 20 (Place in Unit 21)
___ Unit 5 (Place in Unit 6)   ___ Unit 23 (Place in Unit 24)
___ Unit 9 (Place in Unit 10)   ___ Unit 29 (Place in Unit 30)
___ Unit 15 (Place in Unit 16)   ___ Unit 38 (Place in *Read Well Plus*)

Blackline Master **49**

Reproducible Student Placement Record, Part 1 and Part 2 Summary available on page 49.

If a student reads 11 or more letter names and/or sounds in subtests A and B, then the student goes on to Subtests C and D.

Sergio read 19 letter names and sounds, so he went on to take Subtests C and D.

If a student reads five or more high-frequency and/or pattern words correctly in Subtests C and D, then the student goes on to Part 2 of the Placement Inventory. Sergio was unable to read any words (scoring 0), so his Placement Inventory is complete. Students who do not go on to Part 2, place in Unit 1. (See the chart on page 26–27.)

Tamela's Example

Warm-Up

Tamela was able to write her first name and last name, using appropriate capital and small letters.

Subtests A and B

Tamela demonstrated knowledge of 26 letter names and 23 sounds. Tamela scored a total of 49 on Subtests A and B, so she was given Subtests C and D.

Subtests C and D

Tamela was able to read 17 high-frequency words and 18 pattern words. Her combined score on Subtests C and D was 35.

Placement Inventory Part 1, Total Score

Tamela's total score was 84. Tamela will go on to Part 2 of the Placement Inventory. Tamela's score on Part 1 may be used to help place her with students who most closely match her skills at the time of testing.

Student Placement Record, Part 1 and Part 2 Summary

Name _____ Tamela Johnson _____ Date _____ Aug 31 _____ Teacher _____ Scott _____

Recommended Placement _____

PART 1

Name Writing Warm-Up

Tamela Johnson

Record a + for each correct response and a – for each incorrect response. On each subtest, stop if the student makes five consecutive errors. Point to the remaining rows and ask the student if he or she knows any other letters, sounds, or words.

Subtest A Letter Names

D +	M +	T +	S +	P +	C +	A +
I +	L +	B +	R +	W +	O +	E –
G +	F +	N +	V +	H +	K +	Z +
U +	Q +	Y +	J +	X +		

26/26

Subtest B Sounds

s +	e +	m +	a +	d +	n +	t +
w +	i +	h +	c +	r +	k +	l +
o +	b (d) –	g +	f +	u +	y –	p +
v +	j +	q –	x –	z +		

23/26

Add the scores for Subtests A and B. Stop if the student scores fewer than 10. Place in Unit A. Proceed to Subtests C and D if the student scores 11 or more.

49/52 Subtests A & B

Subtest C High-Frequency Words

the	+	in	+	he	+	as	+
of	–	is	+	for	–	with	+
and	+	you	+	was	+	his	+
a	+	that	+	on	+	they	–
to	+	it	+	are	+	at	+

17/20

Subtest D Pattern Words

see	+	than	+	can	+	start	–
me	+	ant	+	read	+	whack	+
am	+	weeds	+	crash	+	rest	+
dad	+	mint	+	kick	+	try	+
seed	+	him	+	noon	+	will	–

18/20

Add the scores for Subtests C and D. Stop if the student's combined score on Subtests C and D is four or fewer. Place the student in Unit 1.

35/40 Subtests C & D

Add the scores for Subtests A, B, C, and D.

84/92 Total Score A–D

Proceed to Part 2 if the student's combined score on Subtests C and D is five or more. (The student is able to read five or more words correctly.)

PART 2—SUMMARY

Record a SP (Strong Pass), P (Pass), WP (Weak Pass) or NP (No Pass). Stop when the student scores a No Pass or a Weak Pass on any given assessment. Go back and place the student one unit higher than the last assessment with a Strong Pass or Pass.

___ Unit 3 (Place in Unit 4) ___ Unit 20 (Place in Unit 21)
___ Unit 5 (Place in Unit 6) ___ Unit 23 (Place in Unit 24)
___ Unit 9 (Place in Unit 10) ___ Unit 29 (Place in Unit 30)
___ Unit 15 (Place in Unit 16) ___ Unit 38 (Place in *Read Well Plus*)

Blackline Master **49**

Reproducible Student Placement Record, Part 1 and Part 2 Summary available on page 49.

If a student reads five or more high-frequency and/or pattern words correctly in Subtests C and D, then the student goes on to Part 2 of the Placement Inventory.

Tamela read 35 words correctly on Subtests C and D, so she will go on and take Part 2 of the inventory.

Placement Inventory Part 2

Administration Guidelines

Part 2 of the Placement Inventory is composed of end-of-unit Decoding and Oral Reading Fluency Assessments. If students score Strong Passes on these assessments, they have the skills to begin midway through *Read Well 1*.

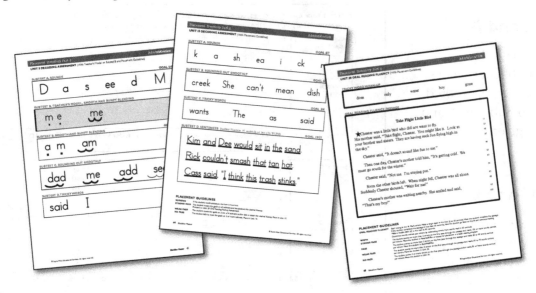

- Administer Part 2 of the Placement Inventory to any child who is able to read five or more high-frequency and/or pattern words on Subtests C and D.
- Use results from Subtest D (Pattern Words) to determine where to begin.

Some students may know several high-frequency words by sight but lack the skills to read pattern words. Such students will place in Unit 1, but will progress rapidly though the early units.

PLACEMENT INVENTORY PART 2: DETERMINING WHERE TO START	
Using the pattern words score from Subtest D	
If the student reads . . .	**Then . . .**
0–4 words correct	Place in Unit 1
5–9 words correct	Begin with Unit 3 Assessment
10–15 words correct	Begin with Unit 5 Assessment
15–20 words correct	Begin with Unit 9 Assessment

When administering the Placement Inventory:

- Assess each child individually, away from others.
- Follow the schedule below until a student scores a Weak Pass or a No Pass on any given assessment.
- Record student responses on the Student Placement Record Part 2.

ADMINISTRATION SCHEDULE		
Administer test for . . .	If the student scores a . . .	Then . . .
Unit 3	No Pass Pass	Place in Unit 1 Administer Unit 5
Unit 5	No Pass Pass	Place in Unit 4 Administer Unit 9
Unit 9	Weak or No Pass Strong Pass	Place in Unit 6 Administer Unit 15
Unit 15	Weak or No Pass Strong Pass	Place in Unit 10 Administer Unit 20
Unit 20	Weak or No Pass Strong Pass	Place in Unit 16 Administer Unit 23
Unit 23	Weak or No Pass Strong Pass	Place in Unit 21 Administer Unit 29
Unit 29	Weak or No Pass Pass or Strong Pass	Place in Unit 24 Administer Unit 38
Unit 38	Weak or No Pass Pass or Strong Pass	Place in Unit 30 Assess for placement in *Read Well Plus*

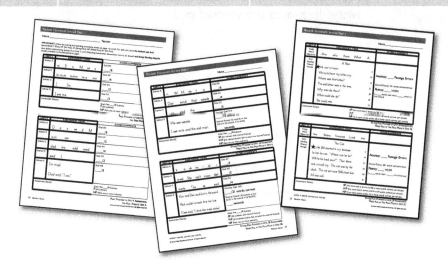

15

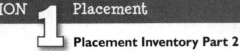

Decoding Assessment Guidelines

Part 2 of the Placement Inventory begins with end-of-the unit Decoding Assessments for Units 3, 5, 9, and 15. These subtests assess a student's skills with letter sounds, Smooth and Bumpy Blending, Sounding Out Smoothly, Tricky Words, and sentence reading. These subtests are scored on the Student Placement Record Part 2. Code errors as shown in the chart.

PROCEDURES AND SCORING FOR ALL SUBTESTS		
If the student . . .	**Then . . .**	**Record . . .**
Needs Assistance	Wait three seconds. Gently tell the student the correct response, draw a line through the item, and write an "A" for "assisted."	Incorrect M d ee s a D̸ ᴬ
Mispronounces	Draw a line through the word. Record what the student said.	Incorrect said was se̸es ˢᵉᵉ
Fails to Blend Smoothly (Smooth and Bumpy Blending Subtest)	If the student fails to blend smoothly—pauses or stops between sounds—draw a line through the item. Rewrite the word and draw dashes between sounds to indicate where the student paused.	Incorrect Seed me add da̸d ᵈ⁻ᵃᵈ
Self-Corrects	If the student spontaneously self-corrects, write "SC," so that you do not count the error. If the student requires more than two attempts, write the words the student said.	Incorrect Correct Does/Dan/Did sun ˢᶜ D̸id Tim sit in the sand?

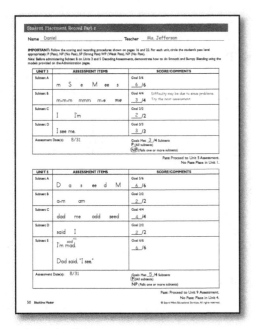

Student Placement Record Part 2 Scoring Sample

Record errors on the Student Placement Record Part 2 while administering the assessment.

Reproducible Student Placement Records Part 2, available on pages 50–54.

From the Unit 6 Assessment forward, time Subtest D in each unit.

TIMED READINGS

As the student begins reading:

1. Start the stopwatch.
2. Be sure to pronounce words not read within three seconds and prompt the student to keep reading.
3. Score as indicated on page 16. However, if a student sounds out a word (whether smooth or bumpy), score as a correct response. Sounding out is reflected in the fluency score.

Transfer assessment scores SP (Strong Pass), P (Pass), WP (Weak Pass), and NP (No Pass) as appropriate onto the Student Placement Record, Part 1 and Part 2 Summary.

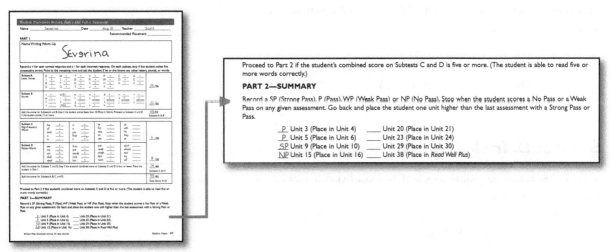

Continue assessing until the student scores a Weak Pass or No Pass. Go back and place the student one unit higher than the last unit with a Strong Pass or Pass. (See chart on page 15.)

How to Administer Units 3 and 5

Record student responses on the Student Placement Record Part 2. The following is a sample script for Unit 5.

Subtest A. Sounds

Tell the student to point under each item and say the sound.
Say something like:

> Point under the first letter. Tell me the first sound. **(/D/)**
> Tell me the next sound. **(/aaa/)**

Subtest B. Smooth and Bumpy Blending

Demonstrate Smooth and Bumpy Blending using the examples on Subtest B. Say something like:

> Watch and listen to me do Bumpy Blending.
> **Touch under each letter.** /m/ . . . /e/ . . .
> Now, watch and listen to me do Smooth Blending.
> **Loop under each letter.** /mmmeee/
> The word is "me."

Following your model, say something like:

> Now you get to do Bumpy Blending.
> You can follow my finger or point by yourself.
>
> Touch the square under the first sound. Do Bumpy Blending. **(/a/ . . . /m/)**
> Now do Smooth Blending. Put your finger at the beginning of the first loop.
> Do Smooth Blending. **(/aaammm/)**
> Tell me the word. **(am)**

Subtest C. Sounding Out Smoothly

Tell the student to do Smooth Blending of each word.
Say something like:

> You get to do Smooth Blending.
> Put your finger at the beginning of the first loop.
> Do Smooth Blending. **(/daaad/)**
> Tell me the word. **(dad)**

Subtest D. Tricky Words

Tell the student to point to each word and read the word.
Say something like:

> Put your finger under the first Tricky Word.
> Tell me the word. **(said)**

Subtest E. Sentences

Tell the student to point to the first word in the sentence and then read the sentence. Say something like:

> You get to read sentences.
> Put your finger under the first word and start when you're ready.

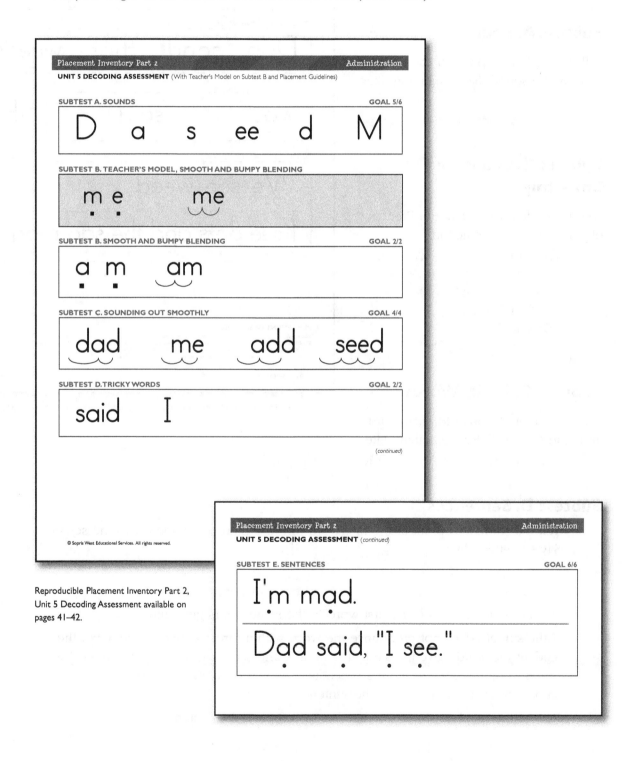

Reproducible Placement Inventory Part 2, Unit 5 Decoding Assessment available on pages 41–42.

How to Administer Units 9 and 15

The following is a sample script for Unit 9.

Subtest A. Sounds

Tell the student to point to each item and say the sound. Say something like:

> Touch under the first letter.
> Read the sound. (/nnn/)

Subtest B. Sounding Out Smoothly

Tell the student to do Smooth Blending of each word. Say something like:

> You get to do Smooth Blending.
> Remember, you want to really stretch out the words.
>
> Do Smooth Blending.
> (/Daaannn/)
> Tell me the word. (Dan)

Subtest C. Tricky Words

Tell the student to point to each word and read the word. Say something like:

> Put your finger under the first Tricky Word. Tell me the word. (was)

Subtest D. Sentences

- Tell the student to point to the first word in the sentence and then read the sentence. Say something like:

    > You get to read sentences.
    >
    > Put your finger under the first word and start when you're ready.

- When the student reads the first word in the sentence, begin timing.

    If the student does not pronounce the word within three seconds, quietly tell the student the word, have the student continue, and score the word as incorrect. Mark errors using the general scoring procedures shown on page 16. Stop timing after the student reads the last word in the sentence.

- Record the number of seconds needed to complete the sentence.

Placement Inventory Part 2   Administration
UNIT 9 DECODING ASSESSMENT (With Placement Guidelines)

SUBTEST A. SOUNDS   GOAL 5/6

n	W	M	ee	t	a

SUBTEST B. SOUNDING OUT SMOOTHLY   GOAL 3/4

Dan   sand   that   weeds

SUBTEST C. TRICKY WORDS   GOAL 3/3

was   said   the

SUBTEST D. SENTENCES   Desired Fluency: 20 seconds or less (30 WCPM)   GOAL 9/10

We see weeds.

I see ants and the sad man.

PLACEMENT GUIDELINES
SCORING   If the student needs assistance, the item is incorrect.
STRONG PASS   The student meets the goals on all subtests and has attained the desired fluency. Proceed to Unit 15 Decoding Assessment.
WEAK PASS   The student meets the goals on 3 out of 4 subtests and/or fails to attain the desired fluency. Place in Unit 6.
NO PASS   The student fails to meet the goals on 2 or more subtests. Place in Unit 6.

© Sopris West Educational Services. All rights reserved.   Blackline Master 43

Reproducible Placement Inventory Part 2, Unit 9 Decoding Assessment available on page 43.

Oral Reading Fluency Guidelines

Part 2 of the Placement Inventory also includes end-of-the-unit Oral Reading Fluency Assessments for Units 20, 23, 29, and 38. These assessments begin with an unscored and untimed Tricky Word Warm-Up, followed by an Oral Reading Fluency Passage scored for accuracy and fluency.

Tricky Word Warm-Up

Have the student point to and read each word. Mark errors on the Student Assessment Record.

Oral Reading Fluency Passage

Passing criteria include two measures for the *same* passage reading.

- Accuracy: Number of errors made for the passage
  The accuracy score provides a measure of a student's informal reading level (independent, instructional, frustration). As passage length increases, students are gradually required to be at an independent level to pass an assessment (98–100% accuracy).

- Oral Reading Fluency: Words correct per minute (WCPM)
  WCPM provides a measure of accuracy and speed. WCPM is the words read in one minute minus errors for that minute.

Administering the Oral Reading Fluency Subtest

1. Have the student read the title. The title provides an unscored warm-up.

2. Start timing the passage at the ★. Mark errors using the diagnostic scoring on page 22. Have the student complete the passage and continue reading for a full 60 seconds.

   - If the student has not completed the passage by the end of 60 seconds, make a single slash (/) at the point the student reached.

   - If the student finishes the passage before 60 seconds have passed, have the student go back to the ★ and keep reading. Stop the student at 60 seconds and make a double slash (//). On the second pass, mark errors differently (e.g., √).

Determining Accuracy and Oral Reading Fluency Scores

1. For the accuracy score, count the number of errors made in the passage.

   - If the student required more than 60 seconds to complete the passage, count errors for the whole passage.

   - If the student read the passage more than once, count errors only for the first time through.

2. For the oral reading fluency score, count the number of words read to the double or single slash. Subtract errors made during the 60-second reading.

DIAGNOSTIC SCORING FOR UNITS 20, 23, 29, AND 38

If the student . . .	Then . . .	Record . . .
Needs Assistance	Wait three seconds. Gently tell the student the correct response, draw a line through the item, and write an "A" for "assisted."	Incorrect We could hear my kitten cr̶y̶. ᴬ
Mispronounces a Word	Draw a line through the item. Record what the student said.	Incorrect that Where was th̶e̶ kitten?
Omits a Word or Word Part	Circle the omission.	Incorrect The (sad) kitten was in the tree.
Inserts a Word	Write what the student said, using a caret to show where the student inserted the word.	Incorrect up Why was she ‸ there?
Self-Corrects	If a student spontaneously self-corrects, write "SC," and score as a correct response.	Correct went/met ᔆᶜ We met at noon.
	If the student requires more than two attempts, score as an incorrect response.	Incorrect went/were/met We m̶e̶t̶ at noon.
Repeats Words	Underline repeated words.	Correct <u>What</u> could she do?
Reverses Words	Draw a line around the words as shown.	Correct She ⌒ could rest.

SECOND TIME THROUGH

Any Error	Make a ✓ over each word	✓ Where was the kitten?

Sylvia and Michael's Examples

Student Placement Record Part 2

Name Sylvia

Sylvia's Score

Sylvia read to the word "do" in one minute (/).

Her passage errors were "met" and "rest."

Sylvia's accuracy score is two passage errors.

To calculate WCPM, only the word "met" is counted as an error as it was made during the one-minute timing. Sylvia read 29 words in one minute minus one error. Her fluency score is 28 WCPM.

UNIT 20		SCORE/COMMENTS
Tricky Word Warm-Up	Are who there What A	
Oral Reading Fluency Passage	A Rest ★We met at noon. *(meet)* — 4 We could hear my kitten cry. — 10 Where was that kitten? — 14 The sad kitten was in the tree. — 21 Why was she there? *(What sc)* — 25 What could she do? / — 29 She could rest. *(sleep)* — 32	Accuracy: _2_ Passage Errors Desired Fluency: 46+ words correct/minute Fluency: _28_ WCPM (_29_ words read minus _1_ errors in one minute)
Assessment Date(s): 8/31	SP (No more than 2 errors and 46 or more words correct per minute.) WP (No more than 2 errors and 36–45 words correct per minute) (NP) (3 or more errors and/or 35 or fewer words correct per minute)	

Strong Pass: Proceed to the Unit 23 Assessment.
Weak Pass or No Pass: Place in Unit 16.

Student Placement Record Part 2

Name Michael A.

Michael's Score

Michael read the whole passage and then went back to the star and read again to "do" in one minute. (//)

Michael made an error on "kitten" the first time he read the passage. His accuracy score is one passage error.

The second time Michael read the passage, he missed "sad" (√). Michael's WCPM is calculated by adding 32 (first reading) plus 29 (second reading) minus the two errors made during the one-minute timing (32+29-2). Michael's fluency score is 59 WCPM.

UNIT 20		SCORE/COMMENTS
Tricky Word Warm-Up	Are who there What A	
Oral Reading Fluency Passage	A Rest ★We met at noon. — 4 We could hear my kitten cry. *(cat)* — 10 Where was that kitten? — 14 The sad kitten was in the tree. √ — 21 Why was she there? *(When sc)* — 25 What could she do? // — 29 She could rest. — 32	Accuracy: _1_ Passage Errors Desired Fluency: 46 + words correct/minute Fluency: _59_ wcpm (_61_ words read minus _2_ errors/minute)
Assessment Date(s): 8/31	(SP) (No more than 2 errors and 46 or more words correct per minute.) WP (No more than 2 errors and 36–45 words correct per minute) NP (3 or more errors and/or 35 or fewer words correct per minute)	

Strong Pass: Proceed to the Unit 23 Assessment.
Weak Pass or No Pass: Place in Unit 16.

Reproducible Student Placement Record available on page 52.

How to Administer Units 20, 23, 29, and 38

The following is a sample script for Unit 38.

Tricky Word Warm-Up

Tell the student to point to each item and say the word. Say something like:

> Touch under the first
> word. Read the word.

Oral Reading Fluency

- Tell the student to point to the first word in the title. Say something like:

> Read the title of the story. What do you think the story is going to be about?

- Have the student point to the first word in the passage. Have the student read the complete passage and continue reading for 60 seconds. Say something like:

> Read the story to me. Please track the words with your finger so I can see where you are reading. Put your finger under the first word. Begin whenever you are ready.

- If time remains at the end of the passage, have the student go back to the ★ and keep reading until 60 seconds have passed. Say something like:

> Wow! Go back to the star and keep reading.

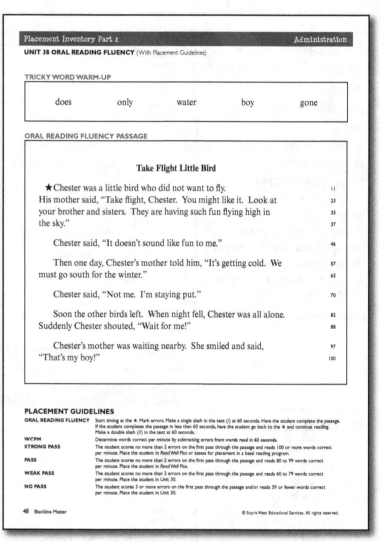

Reproducible Placement Inventory Part 2, Unit 38 available on page 48.

As the student reads, code any errors using the general scoring procedures shown on page 22.

Note: Because the student is being timed, it is important to pronounce any word not identified within three seconds. Quietly tell the student the word, have the student continue, and score the word as incorrect.

Emily's Example

Name __Emily S.__

UNIT 38	ASSESSMENT ITEMS					SCORE/COMMENTS
Tricky Word Warm-Up	does	only	water	boy	gone	

Oral Reading Fluency Passage

Take Flight Little Bird

★ Chester was a little bird who did not want to fly.	11
His mother said, "Take flight, Chester. You might like it. Look at	23
your brother and sisters. They are having such fun flying high in	35
the sky."	37
Chester said, "It doesn't sound like fun to me." //	46
Then one day, Chester's mother told him, "It's getting cold. We	57
must go south for the winter."	63
Chester said, "Not me. I'm staying put."	70
Soon the other birds left. When night fell, Chester was all alone.	82
Suddenly Chester shouted, "Wait for me!"	88
Chester's mother was waiting nearby. She smiled and said,	97
"That's my boy!"	100

Accuracy: _2_
Passage Errors

Desired Fluency: 100 + words correct/minute

Fluency: _143_ WCPM

(_146_ words read minus _3_ errors in one minute)

Assessment Date(s): 8/31

SP (No more than 2 errors and 100 or more words correct per minute)
P (No more than 2 errors and 80 to 99 words correct per minute)
WP (No more than 2 errors and 60 to 79 words correct per minute)
NP (3 or more errors and/or 59 or fewer words correct per minute)

Strong Pass or Pass: Place the student in *Read Well Plus* or assess for placement in a basal reading program.
Weak Pass or No Pass: Place in Unit 30.

WCPM = words correct per minute

Reproducible Student Placement Record Part 2, Unit 38 available on page 54.

Name __Emily Sellers__ Date __Aug 31__ Teacher __Scott__

Recommended Placement _____

PART 1

Name Writing Warm-Up

Emily Sellers

Record a + for each correct response and a – for each incorrect response. On each subtest, stop if the student makes five consecutive errors. Point to the remaining rows and ask the student if he or she knows any other letters, sounds, or words.

Subtest A Letter Names

D	+	M	+	T	+	S	+	P	+	C	+	A	+
I	+	L	+	B	+	R	+	W	+	O	+	E	+
G	+	F	+	N	+	V	+	H	+	K	+	Z	+
U	+	Q	+	Y	+	J	+	X	+				

26 /26

Subtest B Sounds

s	+	e	+	m	+	a	+	d	+	n	+	t	+
w	+	i	+	h	+	c	+	r	+	k	+	l	+
o	+	b	+	g	+	f	+	u	+	y	+	p	+
v	+	j	+	q	+	x	+	z	+				

26 /26

Add the scores for Subtests A and B. Stop if the student scores fewer than 10. Place in Unit A. Proceed to Subtests C and D if the student scores 11 or more.

52 /52
Subtests A & B

Subtest C High-Frequency Words

the	+	in	+	he	+	as	+
of	+	is	+	for	+	with	+
and	+	you	+	was	+	his	+
a	+	that	+	on	+	they	+
to	+	it	+	are	+	at	+

20 /20

Subtest D Pattern Words

see	+	than	+	can	+	start	+
me	+	ant	+	read	+	whack	+
am	+	weeds	+	crash	+	rest	+
dad	+	mint	+	kick	+	try	+
seed	+	him	+	noon	+	will	+

20 /20

Add the scores for Subtests C and D. Stop if the student's combined score on Subtests C and D is four or fewer. Place in Unit 1.

40 /40
Subtests C & D

Add the scores for Subtests A, B, C, and D.

92 /92
Total Score A–D

Proceed to Part 2 if the student's combined score on Subtests C and D is five or more. (The student is able to read five or more words correctly.)

PART 2—SUMMARY

Record a SP (Strong Pass), P (Pass), WP (Weak Pass) or NP (No Pass). Stop when the student scores a No Pass or a Weak Pass on any given assessment. Go back and place the student one unit higher than the last assessment with a Strong Pass or Pass.

___ Unit 3 (Place in Unit 4)	_SP_ Unit 20 (Place in Unit 21)
___ Unit 5 (Place in Unit 6)	_SP_ Unit 23 (Place in Unit 24)
___ Unit 9 (Place in Unit 10)	_SP_ Unit 29 (Place in Unit 30)
_SP_ Unit 15 (Place in Unit 16)	_SP_ Unit 38 (Place in *Read Well Plus*)

Reproducible Student Placement Record, Part 1 and Part 2 Summary available on page 49.

Summary of
Placement Inventory Procedures

Placement Inventory Part 1

Administer the Placement Inventory Part 1 to all students.

SUBTEST A (LETTER NAMES) AND SUBTEST B (SOUNDS)	
If the student scores . . .	**Then . . .**
10 or fewer	Stop the assessment and place in Unit A (Intervention)
11 or more	Continue with Subtests C and D

SUBTEST C (HIGH-FREQUENCY WORDS) AND SUBTEST D (PATTERN WORDS)	
If the student scores . . .	**Then . . .**
4 or fewer	Stop the assessment and place in Unit 1
5 or more	Continue with Part 2

Placement Inventory Part 2

Use results from Subtest D (Pattern Words) to determine where to begin.

SUBTEST D (PATTERN WORDS)	
If the student scores . . .	**Then . . .**
0–4 words correct	Stop the assessment and place in Unit 1
5–9 words correct	Begin with Unit 3 Assessment
10–15 words correct	Begin with Unit 5 Assessment
15–20 words correct	Begin with Unit 9 Assessment

ADMINISTRATION AND PLACEMENT SCHEDULE		
Administer test for . . .	**If the student scores a . . .**	**Then . . .**
Unit 3	No Pass Pass	Place in Unit 1 Administer Unit 5
Unit 5	No Pass Pass	Place in Unit 4 Administer Unit 9
Unit 9	Weak or No Pass Strong Pass	Place in Unit 6 Administer Unit 15
Unit 15	Weak or No Pass Strong Pass	Place in Unit 10 Administer Unit 20
Unit 20	Weak or No Pass Strong Pass	Place in Unit 16 Administer Unit 23
Unit 23	Weak or No Pass Strong Pass	Place in Unit 21 Administer Unit 29
Unit 29	Weak or No Pass Pass or Strong Pass	Place in Unit 24 Administer Unit 38
Unit 38	Weak or No Pass Pass or Strong Pass	Place in Unit 30 Assess for placement in *Read Well Plus*

Placing Students

Preliminary Decisions

Once all students have been assessed, preliminary placements can be made. To be successful, young children need instruction that is individually appropriate. This requires multiple placement options *and* sufficient amounts of instructional time.

Groups vary in size. Some groups may be as large as 10 students; others may be as small as three. Whether a group is large or small, there will be a range of student skills within each group, but, the smaller the range, the better. A group of 10 students with similar skill levels is preferable to a group of three students with divergent skills.

- Determine whether you will group across grade levels, within grade levels, or only within your room. Collaboration is the key to providing every child with developmentally appropriate placement options *and* sufficient amounts of instructional time. If instruction is provided solely by a classroom teacher, the progress of all students will be restricted.

DEVELOP A COLLABORATIVE READING SCHEDULE

If your school is struggling with how to provide a well-staffed reading block, the following variables are important to consider:

a. With administrative leadership, designate uninterrupted reading blocks for each grade level.

b. Collaborate with staff to set up a walk-to-read or a modified walk-to-read.

c. Schedule special education, reading specialist, and Title staff into those blocks of time.

d. Recruit staff members as needed to instruct as many groups as possible.

e. Develop procedures for sharing assessment results, regrouping frequently, and sharing instructional strategies.

- Determine how many groups your instructional team can teach. Each group needs a minimum of 30 minutes of teacher-directed instruction, five days per week. Low-performing students require a minimum of 60 minutes of teacher-directed instruction in one or two sessions each day. Students with special needs may require additional time. (See *Getting Started: A Guide to Implementation* for information about scheduling and collaboration.)

PLACEMENT GUIDELINES

Place Students Appropriately—Within each group, the smaller the range of student skills, the better.

Teach Collaboratively—Multiple group options allow you to provide individually appropriate instruction and sufficient amounts of instructional time.

Grouping Students

1. Sort the students' Placement Inventory Records into sets according to where they place (Units A, 1, 4, 6, 10, 16, 24, 30 or *Read Well Plus*).

2. Within each set, sort the Placement Inventory Records from high to low, based on the total scores for Part 1 from high to low (e.g., Unit 1, total score 40; Unit 1, total score 36; Unit 1, total score 35; Unit 1, total score 30).

3. Make a copy of the Group Placement form on page 55. Record student names by unit placement, and then by total scores from highest to lowest.

4. Using the ranked scores from the Group Placement form, divide students into groups based on the number of instructors available.

5. Determine where to begin instruction. For each group, start instruction at the lowest student's placement level. For example, if you have a group of six students that includes four students who placed in Unit 10 and two students who placed in Unit 6, begin instruction in Unit 6.

6. Once instruction has begun, adjust groupings frequently to meet the needs of individual students.

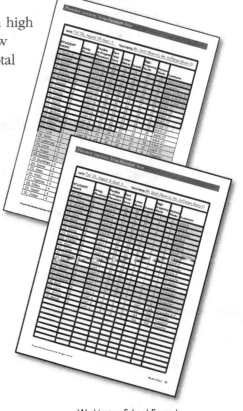

Washington School Example
See pages 32–33.

Washington School's Example—
First Grade Collaboration

Washington School is located in a high-risk neighborhood. The staff at Washington has made a strong professional commitment to helping all children read well. Decisions regarding curricula are research based. Decisions about scheduling, staffing, and intervention are based on the knowledge that student success in a high-risk population rests in the hands of a coordinated staff effort. The staff is committed to the following:

- Use of *Read Well K* in kindergarten
- Use of *Read Well 1* and *Read Well Plus* in first grade
- Use of *Read Well 1* and *Read Well Plus* in second grade as needed
- Use of *Read Well 1* and *Read Well Plus* as needed for remediation in third grade
- Staff training and coaching in *Read Well*
- A one-hour, protected reading block for each grade level
- Scheduled time with Title I and special education staff during the reading block

Staffing and Scheduling Decisions

The hour from 10:00 A.M. to 11:00 A.M. is a scheduled, uninterrupted reading time for the first grade. During this time, the classroom staff, Title I, and special education staff provide concentrated small group instruction. Staff has agreed to implement a Walk-to-Read model with grouping between classrooms. A Title I paraprofessional is also free to provide an additional 30 minutes of tutoring or group instruction to first grade students later in the day.

The instructional team meets every other week for the first two months of school and then every third week to discuss assessment results and placement.

Administering the Placement Inventory

The Title I teacher and paraprofessional, special education teacher, and two first grade paraprofessionals administer the Placement Inventory to all first grade students during the first and second week of school. During this time, the classroom teachers provide whole class instruction in *Read Well 1* Units 1 and 2.

Results

The Title 1 and special education staff complete the Placement Inventories, sort them, and complete the Group Placement form. See the completed Group Placement forms on pages 32 and 33. The team will make final grouping decisions.

SUMMARY OF RESULTS	
Number of Students	**Placement**
1	*Read Well Plus*
2	Unit 30
3	Unit 21
7	Unit 16
17	Unit 10
5	Unit 6
2	Unit 4
11	Unit 1
4	Unit A

Resources

Seven instructors are available to teach groups for the reading block. Each paraprofessional will work with a classroom teacher or the Title I teacher.

Mr. Scott	First Grade Teacher	Room 6
Mrs. West	First Grade Paraprofessional	Room 6
Ms. Jefferson	First Grade Teacher	Room 8
Mr. Martinez and Mrs. Rowland	Librarian and Principal	Room 8
Mrs. Wong	Title I Teacher	Room 15
Mrs. Weber	Title I Paraprofessional	Room 15
Mr. Matthews	Special Education Teacher	Room 16

CREATIVE STAFFING

Mr. Martinez, the librarian, and Mrs. Rowland, the principal, have decided to share a first grade reading group. Each will teach the group two to three days per week.

Washington is an example based on real schools. Librarians have taught *Read Well* groups and report many positive effects related to the coordination of *Read Well* and the library program. Principals in many schools have shared the responsibility of teaching a *Read Well* group and report that the experience was the highlight of each day.

Placement Inventory, Group Placement Form

DATE Fall '06, August 28–Sept. 6				TEACHER(S) Mr. Scott (Room 6), Ms. Jefferson (Room 8)				
STUDENT NAME	Group Placement	Possible In-Program Placement	Part Total Score	Letter Names	Sounds	High-Frequency Words	Pattern Words	Comments
1. Emily S.	1	RW1 +	92	26	26	20	20	RWK-20/RW1-32
2. Hannah	1	Unit 30	92	26	26	20	20	Transfer
3. Carlos	1	Unit 30	91	26	25	20	19	RWK-20/RW1-32
4. Jamal	1	Unit 21	86	26	25	16	19	RWK-20/RW1-32
5. Andrew	1	Unit 21	83	25	23	15	20	RWK-20/RW1-32
6. Michael A.	1	Unit 21	86	26	26	14	20	RWK-17
7. Tamela	2	Unit 16	84	26	23	17	18	RWK-17
8. Dominic	2	Unit 16	74	26	26	10	12	RWK-17
9. Paulino	2	Unit 16	79	26	25	14	14	RWK-17
10. Amira	2	Unit 16	78	26	24	13	15	RWK-17
11. Sylvia	2	Unit 16	77	26	23	14	13	RWK-17
12. Steven	2	Unit 16	77	26	24	12	15	RWK-17
13. Bethany	2	Unit 16	70	25	20	12	13	RWK-17
14. Makaila	3	Unit 10	78	26	25	12	15	RWK-17
15. Bianca	3	Unit 10	70	26	24	10	12	RWK-17
16. Tyrone	3	Unit 10	69	26	25	9	9	Transfer
17. Tyler	3	Unit 10	69	26	24	10	9	RWK-12
18. Dylan	3	Unit 10	66	26	22	8	10	RWK-12
19. LaMarcus	3	Unit 10	68	26	25	8	9	RWK-12
20. Lacie	3	Unit 10	65	25	24	8	8	RWK-12
21. Angus	3	Unit 10	62	26	23	6	7	RWK-12
22. Severina	3	Unit 10	59	25	20	6	8	RWK-12
23. Guadelupe	4	Unit 10	52	26	19	6	8	RWK-12
24. Daniel	4	Unit 10	52	26	22	7	7	RWK-12
25. Anna	4	Unit 10	50	21	15	6	8	RWK-12
26. Andy	4	Unit 10	46	20	12	6	8	RWK-12
27. Jasmine	4	Unit 10	45	22	11	5	7	RWK-12
28. Dillon	4	Unit 10	47	22	11	6	8	RWK-12
29. Yassir	4	Unit 10	44	20	10	6	8	Transfer
30. Jadae	4	Unit 10	40	18	10	6	6	RWK-12

The shaded bands show preliminary groups formed by the instructional team.

continued

Blackline Master 55

Reproducible Placement Inventory, Group Placement form available on page 55.

Note: "RWK" refers to *Read Well K* instruction in kindergarten with the last unit passed. Students 1, 3, 4, and 5 completed *Read Well K* and Units 21–32 of *Read Well 1* in kindergarten.

Placement Inventory, Group Placement Form

DATE <u>Fall '06, August 8–Sept. 6</u>   TEACHER(S) <u>Mr. Scott (Room 6), Ms. Jefferson (Room 8)</u>

STUDENT NAME	Group Placement	Possible In-Program Placement	Part Total Score	Letter Names	Sounds	High-Frequency Words	Pattern Words	Comments
31. Cho	5	Unit 6	41	15	18	3	5	RWK-8
32. Tanya	5	Unit 6	38	18	12	3	5	RWK-8
33. Michael T.	5	Unit 4	51	26	20	3	2	Transfer
34. Carole	5	Unit 4	33	17	11	3	2	RWK-8
35. Jana	5	Unit 4	31	16	12	1	2	RWK-8
36. Roxie	5	Unit 4	31	18	9	1	2	RWK-8
37. Candace	5	Unit 4	23	10	10	1	2	RWK (Spring)
38. Emma	6	Unit 1	37	25	12	0	0	RWK-5
39. Roberto	6	Unit 1	35	25	10	0	0	RWK-5
40. Shelley	6	Unit 1	28	26	0	1	2	Transfer
41. Mary	6	Unit 1	26	18	5	1	2	RWK-5
42. Juana	6	Unit 1	21	12	7	1	1	Transfer
43. Sebastian	6	Unit 1	21	13	6	1	1	Transfer
44. Elaine	6	Unit 1	20	13	6	1	0	Transfer
45. Sergio	7	Unit 1	19	16	3	0	0	Transfer
46. Daniel	7	Unit 1	11	11	0	0	0	Transfer
47. Emily N.	7	Unit 1	11	10	1	0	0	Transfer
48. Christopher	7	Unit 1	12	12	0	0	0	Transfer
49. Mark	8	Unit A	8	6	2	NA*	NA	Preludes A–F
50. Lacie	8	Unit A	0	0	0	NA	NA	Transfer
51. Arturo	8	Unit A	0	0	0	NA	NA	Transfer
52. Melinda	8	Unit A	0	0	0	NA	NA	Transfer

Blackline Master **55**

Reproducible Placement Inventory, Group Placement form available on page 55.

* NA=Not Applicable
Subtests for high-frequency words and pattern words were not administered.

Decision Making

At the end of the second week of school, the classroom teachers and specialists meet to place students in their initial groups. As the teachers make decisions, they weigh and balance the following factors:

- Amount of instructional time per group based on needs—the lowest-performing students require the most instructional time.

- Range of skills in a group—no child should ever be placed higher than the Placement Inventory results indicate.

- Size of group—the lowest-performing groups are kept the smallest.

Preliminary placements are made as follows:

Room 6	Mr. Scott and Mrs. West	
Group 1	6 students	Start at Unit 21 (one student placed in *RW Plus*, two in Unit 30, three in Unit 21)
Group 2	7 students	Start at Unit 16 (seven students placed at Unit 16)
Group 3	9 students	Start at Unit 10 (nine students placed at Unit 10)
Room 8	Ms. Jefferson and Mr. Martinez/Mrs. Rowland	
Group 5	7 students	Start at Unit 4 (two students placed at Unit 6, five students at Unit 4)
Group 7	4 students	Start at Unit 1 (four students placed at Unit 1)
Title 1 Room	Mrs. Wong and Mrs. Weber	
Group 4	8 students	Start at Unit 10 (eight students placed at Unit 10)
Group 6	7 students	Start at Unit 1 (seven students placed at Unit 1)
Special Education	Mr. Matthews	
Group 8	4 students	Start at Unit A

Staff anticipates groups to change with some students moving up rapidly in response to teacher-directed instruction.

Daily Instructional Schedule

Room 6: Mr. Scott and Mrs. West

Mr. Scott (classroom teacher) and Mrs. West (paraprofessional) are assigned the three most mature and capable of the groups. Mr. Scott and Mrs. West work out the following routine, alternating groups.

10:00 – 10:30	Group 1, Teacher-Directed Instruction Group 2, Independent Work	Mr. Scott
10:00 – 10:40	Group 3, Teacher-Directed Instruction	Mrs. West
10:30 – 11:00	Group 2, Teacher-Directed Instruction Group 1, Independent Work	Mr. Scott
10:40 – 11:00	Group 3, Independent Work While Group 3 is working independently, Mrs. West is free to give assessments, listen to individuals read (checkouts), and provide tutorials (for students moving up a group and for students struggling to keep up with their group).	

One student, Emily H., has placed out of *Read Well*. As a shy first grader, Emily is unsure of new situations. Though Emily reads fluently at a second grade reading level, her parents and teacher wish her to remain in the first grade reading program. During reading group, Emily will read the teacher text. During independent work, Emily will be given alternative assignments—including sustained silent reading in a literature book.

Room 8: Ms. Jefferson and Mr. Martinez/Mrs. Rowland
Title 1 Room: Mrs. Wong and Mrs. Weber

Each instructional team will share two groups. Each group will receive 45–50 minutes of direct instruction followed by 10–15 minutes of independent work and Partner Reading. While students work independently, the instructors will administer assessments, listen to individuals read (checkouts), and provide tutorials.

Note: The first grade team avoids sending two low groups to one room. Though children will be instructed in their appropriate groups, the staff hopes to decrease possible labeling and increase student motivation and responsibility.

Special Education: Mr. Matthews

Mr. Matthews takes the four lowest-performing students. These students will also be given extra practice each afternoon with the Title I paraprofessional.

SECTION 2

Placement Inventory and Forms

This section includes the **Placement Inventory** and recordkeeping forms.

Permission to reprint the Placement Inventory forms is provided on the copyright page of this manual.

36

NAME WRITING WARM-UP

SUBTEST A. LETTER NAMES

D M T S P C A

I L B R W O E

G F N V H K Z

U Q Y J X

Blackline Master **37**

SUBTEST B. SOUNDS

s   e   m   a   d   n   t

w   i   h   c   r   k   l

o   b   g   f   u   y   p

v   j   q   x   z

SUBTEST C. HIGH-FREQUENCY WORDS

the	in	he	as
of	is	for	with
and	you	was	his
a	that	on	they
to	it	are	at

SUBTEST D. PATTERN WORDS

see	than	can	start
me	ant	read	whack
am	weeds	crash	rest
dad	mint	kick	try
seed	him	noon	will

UNIT 3 DECODING ASSESSMENT (With Teacher's Model on Subtest B)

SUBTEST A. SOUNDS　　　　　　　　　　　　　　　　　　　**GOAL 5/6**

m　　S　　e　　M　　ee　　　s

SUBTEST B. TEACHER'S MODEL, SMOOTH AND BUMPY BLENDING　　　**GOAL 4/4**

SUBTEST B. SMOOTH AND BUMPY BLENDING　　　　　　　　**GOAL 4/4**

m m m　　mmm　　m e　　me

SUBTEST C. TRICKY WORD (AND I'M)　　　　　　　　　　　**GOAL 2/2**

I　　　I'm

SUBTEST D. SENTENCES　　　　　　　　　　　　　　　　　**GOAL 3/3**

I see me.

PLACEMENT GUIDELINES

SCORING	If the student needs assistance, the item is incorrect.
PASS	The student meets the goals on all subtests. Proceed to Unit 5 Decoding Assessment.
NO PASS	The student fails to meet the goals on 1 or more subtests. Place in Unit 1.

UNIT 5 DECODING ASSESSMENT (With Teacher's Model on Subtest B and Placement Guidelines)

SUBTEST A. SOUNDS　　　　　　　　　　　　　　　　　　　　GOAL 5/6

D　a　s　ee　d　M

SUBTEST B. TEACHER'S MODEL, SMOOTH AND BUMPY BLENDING

SUBTEST B. SMOOTH AND BUMPY BLENDING　　　　　　　　　GOAL 2/2

SUBTEST C. SOUNDING OUT SMOOTHLY　　　　　　　　　　　GOAL 4/4

　　me　add　

SUBTEST D. TRICKY WORDS　　　　　　　　　　　　　　　　GOAL 2/2

said　I

(continued)

　　　　　　Blackline Master　41

UNIT 5 DECODING ASSESSMENT (continued)

SUBTEST E. SENTENCES   GOAL 6/6

I'm mad.

Dad said, "I see."

PLACEMENT GUIDELINES

SCORING   If the student needs assistance, the item is incorrect.
PASS   The student meets the goals on all subtests. Proceed to Unit 9 Decoding Assessment.
NO PASS   The student fails to meet the goals on 1 or more subtests. Place in Unit 4.

UNIT 9 DECODING ASSESSMENT (With Placement Guidelines)

SUBTEST A. SOUNDS   GOAL 5/6

n W M ee t a

SUBTEST B. SOUNDING OUT SMOOTHLY   GOAL 3/4

Dan sand that weeds

SUBTEST C. TRICKY WORDS   GOAL 3/3

was said the

SUBTEST D. SENTENCES Desired Fluency: 20 seconds or less (30 WCPM)   GOAL 9/10

We see weeds.

I see ants and the sad man.

PLACEMENT GUIDELINES

SCORING	If the student needs assistance, the item is incorrect.
STRONG PASS	The student meets the goals on all subtests and has attained the desired fluency. Proceed to Unit 15 Decoding Assessment.
WEAK PASS	The student meets the goals on 3 out of 4 subtests and/or fails to attain the desired fluency. Place in Unit 6.
NO PASS	The student fails to meet the goals on 2 or more subtests. Place in Unit 6.

UNIT 15 DECODING ASSESSMENT (With Placement Guidelines)

SUBTEST A. SOUNDS   GOAL 6/7

> k   a   sh   ea   i   ck   r

SUBTEST B. SOUNDING OUT SMOOTHLY   GOAL 4/5

> creek   She   can't   mean   dish

SUBTEST C. TRICKY WORDS   GOAL 3/4

> wants   The   as   said

SUBTEST D. SENTENCES Desired Fluency: 35 seconds or less (36 WCPM)   GOAL 19/21

> Kim and Dee would sit in the sand.
>
> Rick couldn't smash that tan hat.
>
> Cass said, "I think this trash stinks."

PLACEMENT GUIDELINES

SCORING	If the student needs assistance, the item is incorrect.
STRONG PASS	The student meets the goals on all subtests and has attained the desired fluency. Proceed to Unit 20 Oral Reading Fluency Assessment.
WEAK PASS	The student meets the goals on 3 out of 4 subtests and/or fails to attain the desired fluency. Place in Unit 10.
NO PASS	The student fails to meet the goals on 2 or more subtests. Place in Unit 10.

UNIT 20 ORAL READING FLUENCY (With Placement Guidelines)

TRICKY WORD WARM-UP

Are	who	there	What	A

ORAL READING FLUENCY PASSAGE

A Rest

★We met at noon.   4

We could hear my kitten cry.   10

Where was that kitten?   14

The sad kitten was in the tree.   21

Why was she there?   25

What could she do?   29

She could rest.   32

PLACEMENT GUIDELINES

ORAL READING FLUENCY	Start timing at the ★. Mark errors. Make a single slash in the text (/) at 60 seconds, but have the student complete the passage. If the student completes the passage in less than 60 seconds, have the student go back to the ★ and continue reading. Make a double slash (//) in the text at 60 seconds.
WCPM	Determine words correct per minute by subtracting errors from words read in 60 seconds.
STRONG PASS	The student scores no more than 2 errors on the first pass through the passage and reads a minimum of 46 or more words correct per minute. Proceed to the Unit 23 Oral Reading Fluency Assessment.
WEAK PASS	The student scores no more than 2 errors on the first pass through the passage and reads 36 to 45 words correct per minute. Place in Unit 16.
NO PASS	The student scores 3 or more errors on the first pass through the passage and/or reads 35 or fewer words correct per minute. Place in Unit 16.

     Blackline Master   45

UNIT 23 ORAL READING FLUENCY (With Placement Guidelines)

TRICKY WORD WARM-UP

two	listens	because	Look	one

ORAL READING FLUENCY PASSAGE

The Cat

★Little Bill started to cry because 6

he lost his cat. "Where can he be? 14

Will he be back soon?" Then there 21

was a small cry. The cat was by the 30

clock. The cat sat near Bill's best bat. 38

All was well. 41

PLACEMENT GUIDELINES

ORAL READING FLUENCY	Start timing at the ★. Mark errors. Make a single slash in the text (/) at 60 seconds. Have the student complete the passage. If the student completes the passage in less than 60 seconds, have the student go back to the ★ and continue reading. Make a double slash (//) in the text at 60 seconds.
WCPM	Determine words correct per minute by subtracting errors from words read in 60 seconds.
STRONG PASS	The student scores no more than 2 errors on the first pass through the passage and reads a minimum of 55 or more words correct per minute. Proceed to the Unit 29 Oral Reading Fluency Assessment.
WEAK PASS	The student scores no more than 2 errors on the first pass through the passage and reads 44 to 54 words correct per minute. Place in Unit 21.
NO PASS	The student scores 3 or more errors on the first pass through the passage and/or reads 43 or fewer words correct per minute. Place in Unit 21.

UNIT 29 ORAL READING FLUENCY (With Placement Guidelines)

TRICKY WORD WARM-UP

| ago | worked | they | your | store |

ORAL READING FLUENCY PASSAGE

The Park

★Grandmother asked me to go to the park.   8
She said, "It's a long way to the park, so I will   20
stop by to get you at noon."   27

We had things to play with and things to eat.   37
What a fun day together!   42

Grandmother said, "Let's get going."   47

I said, "I do not want to go, but I understand that   59
we must."   61

PLACEMENT GUIDELINES

ORAL READING FLUENCY	Start timing at the ★. Mark errors. Make a single slash in the text (/) at 60 seconds. Have the student complete the passage. If the student completes the passage in less than 60 seconds, have the student go back to the ★ and continue reading. Make a double slash (//) in the text at 60 seconds.
WCPM	Determine words correct per minute by subtracting errors from words read in 60 seconds.
STRONG PASS	The student scores no more than 2 errors on the first pass through the passage and reads a minimum of 74 or more words correct per minute. Proceed to the Unit 38 Oral Reading Fluency Assessment.
PASS	The student scores no more than 2 errors on the first pass through the passage and reads 62 to 73 words correct per minute. Proceed to the Unit 38 Oral Reading Fluency Assessment.
WEAK PASS	The student scores no more than 2 errors on the first pass through the passage and reads 51 to 61 words correct per minute. Place in Unit 24.
NO PASS	The student scores 3 or more errors on the first pass through the passage and/or reads 50 or fewer words correct per minute. Place in Unit 24.

UNIT 38 ORAL READING FLUENCY (With Placement Guidelines)

TRICKY WORD WARM-UP

does	only	water	boy	gone

ORAL READING FLUENCY PASSAGE

Take Flight Little Bird

★Chester was a little bird who did not want to fly.   11
His mother said, "Take flight, Chester. You might like it. Look at   23
your brother and sisters. They are having such fun flying high in   35
the sky."   37

Chester said, "It doesn't sound like fun to me."   46

Then one day, Chester's mother told him, "It's getting cold. We   57
must go south for the winter."   63

Chester said, "Not me. I'm staying put."   70

Soon the other birds left. When night fell, Chester was all alone.   82
Suddenly Chester shouted, "Wait for me!"   88

Chester's mother was waiting nearby. She smiled and said,   97
"That's my boy!"   100

PLACEMENT GUIDELINES

ORAL READING FLUENCY	Start timing at the ★. Mark errors. Make a single slash in the text (/) at 60 seconds. Have the student complete the passage. If the student completes the passage in less than 60 seconds, have the student go back to the ★ and continue reading. Make a double slash (//) in the text at 60 seconds.
WCPM	Determine words correct per minute by subtracting errors from words read in 60 seconds.
STRONG PASS	The student scores no more than 2 errors on the first pass through the passage and reads 100 or more words correct per minute. Place the student in *Read Well Plus* or assess for placement in a basal reading program.
PASS	The student scores no more than 2 errors on the first pass through the passage and reads 80 to 99 words correct per minute. Place the student in *Read Well Plus*.
WEAK PASS	The student scores no more than 2 errors on the first pass through the passage and reads 60 to 79 words correct per minute. Place the student in Unit 30.
NO PASS	The student scores 3 or more errors on the first pass through the passage and/or reads 59 or fewer words correct per minute. Place the student in Unit 30.

Name _____Date _____ Teacher _____

Recommended Placement _____

PART 1

Name Writing Warm-Up

Record a + for each correct response and a – for each incorrect response. On each subtest, stop if the student makes five consecutive errors. Point to the remaining rows and ask the student if he or she knows any other letters, sounds, or words.

Subtest A Letter Names	D ____ M ____ T ____ S ____ P ____ C ____ A ____ I ____ L ____ B ____ R ____ W ____ O ____ E ____ G ____ F ____ N ____ V ____ H ____ K ____ Z ____ U ____ Q ____ Y ____ J ____ X ____	____/26
Subtest B Sounds	s ____ e ____ m ____ a ____ d ____ n ____ t ____ w ____ i ____ h ____ c ____ r ____ k ____ l ____ o ____ b ____ g ____ f ____ u ____ y ____ p ____ v ____ j ____ q ____ x ____ z ____	____/26
Add the scores for Subtests A and B. Stop if the student scores fewer than 10. Place in Unit A. Proceed to Subtests C and D if the student scores 11 or more.		____/52 Subtests A & B

Subtest C High-Frequency Words	the _____ in _____ he _____ as _____ of _____ is _____ for _____ with _____ and _____ you _____ was _____ his _____ a _____ that _____ on _____ they _____ to _____ it _____ are _____ at _____	____/20
Subtest D Pattern Words	see _____ than _____ can _____ start _____ me _____ ant _____ read _____ whack _____ am _____ weeds _____ crash _____ rest _____ dad _____ mint _____ kick _____ try _____ seed _____ him _____ noon _____ will _____	____/20
Add the scores for Subtests C and D. Stop if the student's combined score on Subtests C and D is four or fewer. Place the student in Unit 1.		____/40 Subtests C & D
Add the scores for Subtests A, B, C, and D.		____/92 Total Score A–D

Proceed to Part 2 if the student's combined score on Subtests C and D is five or more. (The student is able to read five or more words correctly.)

PART 2—SUMMARY

Record a SP (Strong Pass), P (Pass), WP (Weak Pass) or NP (No Pass). Stop when the student scores a No Pass or a Weak Pass on any given assessment. Go back and place the student one unit higher than the last assessment with a Strong Pass or Pass.

___ Unit 3 (Place in Unit 4)   ___ Unit 20 (Place in Unit 21)
___ Unit 5 (Place in Unit 6)   ___ Unit 23 (Place in Unit 24)
___ Unit 9 (Place in Unit 10) ___ Unit 29 (Place in Unit 30)
___ Unit 15 (Place in Unit 16) ___ Unit 38 (Place in Read Well Plus)

Name _____ Teacher _____

IMPORTANT: Follow the scoring and recording procedures shown on pages 16 and 22. For each unit, circle the student's pass level appropriately: P (Pass), NP (No Pass), SP (Strong Pass) WP (Weak Pass), NP (No Pass).

Note: Before administering Subtest B on Units 3 and 5 Decoding Assessments, demonstrate how to do Smooth and Bumpy Blending using the models provided on the Administration pages.

UNIT 3	ASSESSMENT ITEMS	SCORE/COMMENTS
Subtest A	m S e M ee s	Goal 5/6 ____/6
Subtest B	m·m·m mmm m·e me	Goal 4/4 ____/4
Subtest C	I I'm	Goal 2/2 ____/2
Subtest D	I see me.	Goal 3/3 ____/3
Assessment Date(s):		Goals Met ____/4 Subtests P (All subtests) NP (Fails one or more subtests)

Pass: Proceed to Unit 5 Assessment.

No Pass: Place in Unit 1.

UNIT 5	ASSESSMENT ITEMS	SCORE/COMMENTS
Subtest A	D a s ee d M	Goal 5/6 ____/6
Subtest B	a·m am	Goal 2/2 ____/2
Subtest C	dad me add seed	Goal 4/4 ____/4
Subtest D	said I	Goal 2/2 ____/2
Subtest E	I'm mad. Dad said, "I see."	Goal 6/6 ____/6
Assessment Date(s):		Goals Met ____/5 Subtests P (All subtests) NP (Fails one or more subtests)

Pass: Proceed to Unit 9 Assessment.

No Pass: Place in Unit 4.

Name_____

UNIT 9	ASSESSMENT ITEMS	SCORE/COMMENTS
Subtest A	n W M ee t a	Goal 5/6 _____/6
Subtest B	Dan sand that weeds	Goal 3/4 _____/4
Subtest C	was said the	Goal 3/3 _____/3
Subtest D	We see weeds. I see ants and the sad man.	Accuracy Goal 9/10 _____/10 words correct Desired Fluency: 20 seconds or less (10/10 in 20 seconds = 30 WCPM) _____ seconds
Assessment Date(s):		Goals Met ____/4 Subtests SP (All subtests with desired fluency) WP (3/4 subtests and/or fails to attain the desired fluency) NP (Fails two or more subtests)

Strong Pass: Proceed to Unit 15 Assessment.
Weak Pass or No Pass: Place in Unit 6.

UNIT 15	ASSESSMENT ITEMS	SCORE/COMMENTS
Subtest A	k a sh ea i ck r	Goal 6/7 _____/7
Subtest B	creek She can't mean dish	Goal 4/5 _____/5
Subtest C	wants The as said	Goal 3/4 _____/4
Subtest D	Kim and Dee would sit in the sand. Rick couldn't smash that tan hat. Cass said, "I think this trash stinks."	Accuracy Goal 19/21 _____/21 words correct Desired Fluency: 35 seconds or less (21/21 in 35 seconds = 36 WCPM) _____ seconds
Assessment Date(s):		Goals Met ____/4 Subtests SP (All subtests with desired fluency) WP (3/4 subtests and/or fails to attain the desired fluency) NP (Fails two or more subtests)

Strong Pass: Proceed to Unit 20 Assessment.
Weak Pass or No Pass: Place in Unit 10.

WCPM = words correct per minute

Name_____

UNIT 20	ASSESSMENT ITEMS	SCORE/COMMENTS
Tricky Word Warm-Up	Are who there What A	
Oral Reading Fluency Passage	A Rest ★ We met at noon. 4 We could hear my kitten cry. 10 Where was that kitten? 14 The sad kitten was in the tree. 21 Why was she there? 25 What could she do? 29 She could rest. 32	Accuracy: _____ Passage Errors Desired Fluency: 46+ words correct/minute Fluency: _____ WCPM (_____ words read minus _____ errors in one minute)

Assessment Date(s):

SP (No more than 2 errors and 46 or more words correct per minute)
WP (No more than 2 errors and 36–45 words correct per minute)
NP (3 or more errors and/or 35 or fewer words correct per minute)

Strong Pass: Proceed to Unit 23 Assessment.
Weak Pass or No Pass: Place in Unit 16.

UNIT 23	ASSESSMENT ITEMS	SCORE/COMMENTS
Tricky Word Warm-Up	two listens because Look one	
Oral Reading Fluency Passage	The Cat ★ Little Bill started to cry because 6 he lost his cat. "Where can he be? 14 Will he be back soon?" Then there 21 was a small cry. The cat was by the 30 clock. The cat sat near Bill's best bat. 38 All was well. 41	Accuracy: _____ Passage Errors Desired Fluency: 55+ words correct/minute Fluency: _____ WCPM (_____ words read – _____ errors/minute)

Assessment Date(s):

SP (No more than 2 errors and 55 or more words correct per minute)
WP (No more than 2 errors and 44 to 54 words correct per minute)
NP (3 or more errors and/or 43 or fewer words correct per minute)

Strong Pass: Proceed to Unit 29 Assessment.
Weak Pass or No Pass: Place in Unit 21.

WCPM = words correct per minute

Name_____

UNIT 29	ASSESSMENT ITEMS	SCORE/COMMENTS
Tricky Word Warm-Up	ago worked they your store	

The Park

Oral Reading Fluency Passage		
★Grandmother asked me to go to the park.	8	
She said, "It's a long way to the park, so I will	20	Accuracy: _____
stop by to get you at noon."	27	Passage Errors
We had things to play with and things to eat.	37	Desired Fluency: 74+ words correct/minute
What a fun day together!	42	Fluency: _____ WCPM
Grandmother said, "Let's get going."	47	(_____ words read minus _____ errors in one minute)
I said, "I do not want to go, but I understand that	59	
we must."	61	

Assessment Date(s):

SP (No more than 2 errors and 74 or more words correct per minute)
P (No more than 2 errors and 62 to 73 words correct per minute)
WP (No more than 2 errors and 51 to 61 words correct per minute)
NP (3 or more errors and/or 50 or fewer words correct per minute)

Strong Pass or Pass: Proceed to Unit 38 Assessment.
Weak Pass or No Pass: Place in Unit 24.

WCPM = words correct per minute

Name_____

UNIT 38	ASSESSMENT ITEMS	SCORE/COMMENTS
Tricky Word Warm-Up	does only water boy gone	

Oral Reading Fluency Passage

Take Flight Little Bird

★ Chester was a little bird who did not want to fly.   11

His mother said, "Take flight, Chester. You might like it. Look at   23

your brother and sisters. They are having such fun flying high in   35

the sky."   37

Chester said, "It doesn't sound like fun to me."   46

Then one day, Chester's mother told him, "It's getting cold. We   57

must go south for the winter."   63

Chester said, "Not me. I'm staying put."   70

Soon the other birds left. When night fell, Chester was all alone.   82

Suddenly Chester shouted, "Wait for me!"   88

Chester's mother was waiting nearby. She smiled and said,   97

"That's my boy!"   100

SCORE/COMMENTS

Accuracy: _____
Passage Errors

Desired Fluency: 100 + words correct/minute

Fluency: _____
WCPM

(_____ words read minus _____ errors in one minute)

Assessment Date(s):

SP (No more than 2 errors and 100 or more words correct per minute)
P (No more than 2 errors and 80 to 99 words correct per minute)
WP (No more than 2 errors and 60 to 79 words correct per minute)
NP (3 or more errors and/or 59 or fewer words correct per minute)

Strong Pass or Pass: Place the student in *Read Well Plus* or assess for placement in a basal reading program.
Weak Pass or No Pass: Place in Unit 30.

WCPM = words correct per minute

DATE _____ TEACHER(S) _____

STUDENT NAME	Group Placement	Possible In-Program Placement	Part Total Score	Letter Names	Sounds	High-Frequency Words	Pattern Words	Comments

SECTION 3

Ongoing Assessment

This section explains how to use end-of-the unit assessments to maximize progress for each child as he or she moves through the program.

Overview

Young children thrive when their lessons are supportive and successful. As each child has a unique background knowledge, response to instruction, and predisposition to reading, it is critical to deliver lessons that are tailored to the needs of each child.

At the end of each unit, it is important to assess each child's progress. *Read Well* Assessments will help you determine whether a child is ready to learn new skills or would benefit from:

- Additional lessons in a unit
- A quick review to firm up past learning
- A slower pace of instruction
- A faster pace of instruction
- Instruction in a different group

ASSESSMENT GUIDELINE

Be faithful in the administration of the assessments.

Frequent assessment is vital to the long-term reading health of each child; therefore, regular assessment is a critical component of *Read Well*.

What Is Assessed

As assessment can cut into instructional time, *Read Well 1* Assessments were designed to quickly measure student mastery of newly introduced skills and to continuously monitor maintenance of previously learned skills. Less frequent but more comprehensive assessment is advisable at the beginning, middle, and end of each school year.

Decoding Assessments— Units A and B (Intervention Units)

These units evaluate:

- Knowledge of sounds
- Knowledge of everyday picture words
- Comprehension (Who is the story about?)

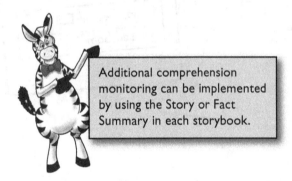

Additional comprehension monitoring can be implemented by using the Story or Fact Summary in each storybook.

Decoding Assessments— Units 1–15

These units evaluate:

- Knowledge of sounds
- Ability to blend sounds smoothly into words
- Knowledge of Tricky Words (words that do not sound out based on sounds taught)
- Sentence reading and fluency

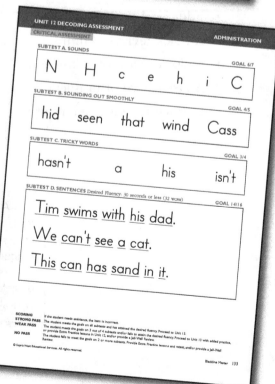

Oral Reading Fluency Assessments—Units 16–38

These units evaluate:

- Knowledge of recently introduced Tricky Words (irregular words)

- Oral reading fluency (words correct per minute)

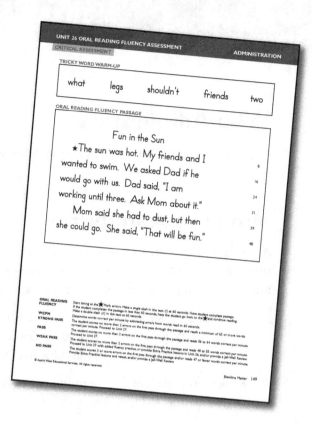

Decoding Diagnoses— Units 23, 26, 28, 30, 34, 36, and 38

Read Well Decoding Diagnoses are for use only with students experiencing difficulty. Use information from both unit assessments and Decoding Diagnoses to identify specific skill deficits. *Read Well* Decoding Diagnoses evaluate knowledge of:

- Sounds
- Vowel discrimination
- Beginning quick sounds
- Blends and word endings
- Tricky Words

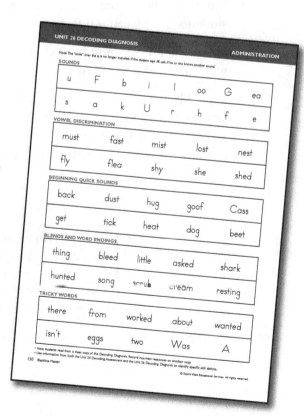

Managing Assessments

Who Administers

Any trained professionals (e.g., paraprofessionals, specialists, and other teachers) can assess students.

When to Administer

Assessments are given at the end of each unit. The assessments can be administered very quickly, requiring only a couple of minutes per student. Assessments can be administered at any time during the school day. Consider options that do not reduce instructional time.

- Arrange a sufficient amount of instructional time per group for instructors to assess their own groups. (See pages 30–35 for a description of a walk-to-read program with one hour of instructional time allocated to each group.)

- Set up a system for identifying when groups will complete a unit. Have a reading coach or floating aides assess individuals while instruction continues.

- Have each homeroom teacher assess students from his or her classroom, even if students are regrouped for reading instruction with a different teacher.

- If options are severely limited, train a volunteer who can work confidentially to assist with informal assessments.

- If possible, assess all students at the end of each unit. Never skip a critical assessment. Critical assessments (Units 4, 8, 10, 12, 15, 19, 23, 26, 28, 30, 34, 36, and 38) are labeled as such. On all other units, assess at least the lowest performing student in any group, any student who has had a Weak Pass in the last two units, and any student who has been absent.

> **INSTRUCTIONAL GUIDELINES**
> One size of reading instruction does not fit all. Regular progress monitoring is critical to meeting the needs of all children.

Balancing Priorities

The time required to administer assessments must be weighed carefully against the potential loss of instructional time. For example, if students have not had *Read Well K* instruction, an average first grade group will easily complete all 38 units of *Read Well 1* by the end of first grade. However, if the teacher stops to assess students one day per week, this same group may only complete up to Unit 28. See passages from each of these units below. The difference in reading levels is visible. This can mean the difference between achieving grade level or not.

Unit 28 Storybook

STORY 2, SOLO

CHAPTER 2
School

Ann asked her grandmother, "What did you do in school?"

Grandmother said, "That was long ago! My friends and I worked hard. We would read and do math."

Ann asked, "Did you do fun things?"

Grandmother said, "Yes, we sang songs, and we ran in the school yard."

Then Grandmother said, "What do you do in school?"

Ann said, "We do fun things too. We sing songs. We read and do math. We run in the school yard."

Grandmother nodded. Then Grandmother said, "I should rest."

What did Ann ask Grandmother Moko? Did Grandmother Moko and her friends work hard in school? What did Ann say she and her friends did in school? What was the same?

Unit 38 Storybook

STORY 3, SOLO

A History of Flight

CHAPTER 1
Hot Air Balloons

What is the title of this story? What does history tell us about? This story is about real things that happened long ago. Do you think the story is fact or fiction?

For thousands of years, people dreamed of traveling in the air like birds, but people had no way to fly. Then about two hundred years ago, two French brothers made a big balloon. They lit a small fire under the balloon and watched as the balloon rose in the air. Soon, their balloon was flying!

Would you like to understand how the hot air balloon could fly? Hot air is lighter than cold air. When the brothers lit the fire, the air inside the balloon got hotter. As the air got hotter, it got lighter, and the balloon began to fly. What do you think happened when the air in the balloon got cold?

The brothers put a rooster, a sheep, and a duck on the first flight of their balloon. Before long, many people rode in hot air balloons.

Who made the first hot air balloon? Pretend your hands are a balloon. Show me what happened to the balloon when the air got hot. Show me what happened when the air got cold. Two hundred years ago, no one had ever ridden in a hot air balloon before. Would you want to be the first one to try it? I think it would make me very nervous. If it didn't work, I wouldn't want anyone to get hurt!

Materials Preparation

1. Make one copy per student of the Student Assessment Record. This form is used to record and score student responses. (You may wish to organize Student Assessment Records in a small group folder or notebook.)

2. Make one copy per group of the Group Assessment Record.

3. Each person who will administer and score assessments should be trained to do so.

4. Assessment administration forms are located in this manual and also at the end of each teacher's guide.

5. Obtain stopwatches. (The assessments for Units 16–38 include measures of oral reading fluency.)

General Administration Guidelines

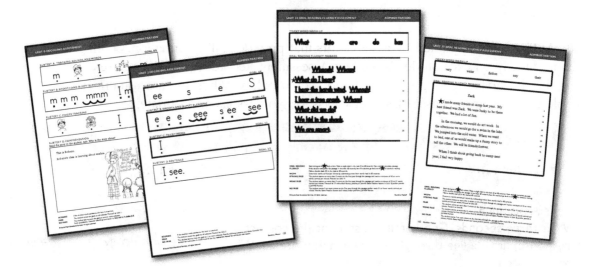

- Assess when students are able to easily complete decoding tasks from the beginning of a lesson. This may occur after two to ten days of instruction in a given unit. (See each teachers guide for sample lessons plans.)

- Assess each child individually where others cannot hear.

- Place the assessment on a desk so that the child can easily point to sounds and words.

- Position yourself so the student cannot see you score.

- Help the child feel comfortable. Most young children enjoy one-to-one time with an adult. Say something like:

    I'm glad I get to listen to you read today.

- Throughout the assessment, compliment the student on things he or she can do.

    You know all the sounds we've practiced. I'm very proud of you.

- Score student responses on the Student Assessment Record, adhering to the scoring criteria on pages 64 and 73.

- As appropriate, record a Strong Pass, Pass, Weak Pass, or No Pass.

Decoding Assessments, Units A-15

Units A–15 are accompanied by assessments that provide skill information. Scoring is done directly on each student's Student Assessment Record. Record responses using the diagnostic scoring explained and shown below. When the assessment is complete, circle Strong Pass, Pass, Weak Pass, or No Pass, as appropriate.

DIAGNOSTIC SCORING FOR UNITS A-15

If the student ...	Record ...
Needs Assistance Wait three seconds. Gently tell the student the correct response, draw a line through the item, and write an "A" for "assisted."	Incorrect She sho~~ul~~d swim in the sea. *(A written above)*
Mispronounces a Word or Sound Draw a line through the item. Record what the student said.	Incorrect would wi~~th~~ wasn't *(was written above wi~~th~~)*
Fails to Blend Smoothly (Smooth and Bumpy Blending Subtest) If the student pauses or stops between sounds, draw a line through the item. Rewrite the word and draw dashes between sounds to indicate where the student paused.	Incorrect sh-e da-sh s~~h~~e Tad can da~~sh~~
Self-Corrects If the student spontaneously self-corrects, write "SC," so that you do not count the error. If the student requires more than two attempts, score as an incorrect response.	Correct Incorrect want *(SC)* Sam/sad/seeds I wish we could see se~~ed~~s.

TIMED SUBTEST

Sentences, Units 6–15

- As the student begins reading, start the stopwatch.
- If a student hesitates on a word for three seconds, pronounce the word and prompt the student to keep reading.
- Score as indicated above. However, if a student sounds out a word (whether smooth or bumpy), score as a correct response. Sounding out is reflected in the fluency score.

Sample Student Assessment Record, Units 13–14

STUDENT ASSESSMENT RECORD

Name _Dylan_

UNIT 13	ASSESSMENT ITEMS	SCORE/COMMENTS
Subtest A	r C a d R ea h	Goal 6/7 _7_ /7
Subtest B	r-at c-an/caaannn r~~a~~t He dim can sweet	Goal 4/5 Needs work on blending with _4_ /5 beginning quick sounds and /r/.
Subtest C	with is w~~a~~nt I'm has	Goal 3/4 _3_ /4
Subtest D	r-an mints The deer ran in the m~~i~~st. Nan meets Sam at the tree. T-ad/Tad Tad didn't eat with me.	Accuracy Goal 15/17 _16_ /17 words correct Desired Fluency: 30 seconds or less (17/17 in 30 seconds = 34 WCPM) _30_ seconds
Assessment Date(s): 10/3		Goals Met _4_ /4 Subtests (SP) (All subtests with desired fluency) WP (3/4 subtests, and/or fails to attain the desired fluency) NP (Fails two or more subtests)

UNIT 14	ASSESSMENT ITEMS	SCORE/COMMENTS
Subtest A	Sh w i r e H c	Goal 6/7 _7_ /7
Subtest B	d-ash r-ead dash him tree Rats read	Goal 4/5 Still needs work on blending. _3_ /5
Subtest C	with should was said w~~a~~nt	Goal 3/4 _3_ /4
Subtest D	sc should She would swim in the sea. We wish we could meet. r-ats/rats tr-eat The rats should eat a sweet treat.	Accuracy Goal 16/18 _18_ /18 words correct Desired Fluency: 30 seconds or less (18/18 in 30 seconds = 36 WCPM) _33_ seconds	If the group is strong, Dylan needs to work with a parapro on blending or be moved to a lower group.
Assessment Date(s): 10/10		Goals Met _3_ /4 Subtests SP (All subtests with desired fluency) (WP) (3/4 subtests, and/or fails to attain the desired fluency) NP (Fails two or more subtests)

    Blackline Master 175

How to Administer Units A and B

Record student's response on the Student Assessment Record, Part 2.
The following is a sample script for Unit A.

Subtest A. Tracking and words

Tell the student to point to each item
and say the picture word or word.

Say something like:

> Touch the dot under the first word. Read the
> word. (I)

> Touch the dot under the next picture word.
> Read the word. (Scissors)

Repeat with "I," {paper}, and "I."

ASSESSMENT GUIDELINES
(Reminder)
When giving an assessment, if you
find yourself helping a student with a
response, score the item as incorrect.
Your assistance means the student
hasn't yet mastered the skill.

Subtest B. Smooth and Bumpy Blending

Have the student touch each square and do
Bumpy Blending.

> You get to do Bumpy Blending.

> Touch the square under the first sound, and do
> Bumpy Blending. (I . . . I . . . I)

Have the student follow the loop and do Smooth Blending.

> Now do Smooth Blending. Put your finger at the beginning
> of the first loop and do Smooth Blending. (/III/)

Subtest C. Finger Tracking

Tell the student to point to each item and say the picture word or word.

Say something like:

> Touch the dot under each word then read each word.

Subtest D. Comprehension

Read the story to the student.

Ask the comprehension question found on the assessment.

Accept any reasonable response.

> General prescriptions are located at the bottom of each assessment.

Mark's Example

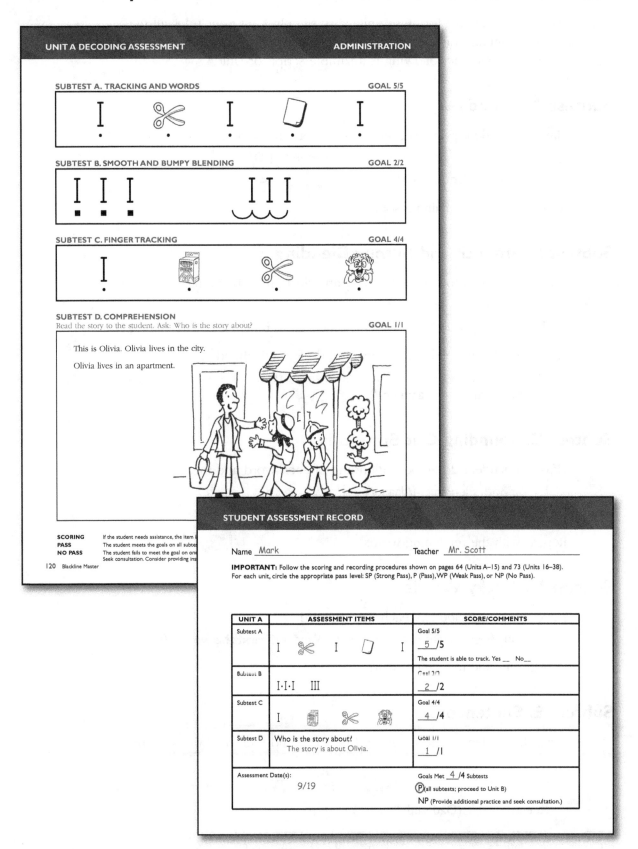

How to Administer Units 1–5

The Decoding Assessments for these units vary slightly. Unit 5 includes all five subtests. While administering assessments, use each individual's Student Assessment Record to mark errors. The following is a sample script for Unit 5.

Subtest A. Sounds

Have the student point to each item and say the sound.

Touch under the first sound. Read the sound. (/D/)

Read the next sound. (/a/)

Repeat with the remaining sounds.

Subtest B. Smooth and Bumpy Blending

Have the student touch each square and do Bumpy Blending.

You get to do Bumpy Blending.

Touch the square under the first sound and do Bumpy Blending. (/a/ . . . /m/ . . .)

Have the student follow the loops and do Smooth Blending.

Now do Smooth Blending. Put your finger at the beginning of the first loop and do Smooth Blending. (/aaammm/)

Subtest C. Sounding Out Smoothly

Have the student do Smooth Blending of each word and then say the word.

Do Smooth Blending. (/daaad/)

Say the word. (dad)

Repeat with the remaining words.

Subtest D. Tricky Words

Have the student identify each Tricky Word.

Put your finger under the first Tricky Word and read the word. (said)

Repeat with the remaining word.

Subtest E. Sentences

Have the student point under the first word and then read the sentence.

You get to read sentences.

Put your finger under the first word and start when you're ready. (I'm mad.)

Keep reading. (Dad said, "I see.")

General prescriptions are located at the bottom of each assessment.

Jana's Example

UNIT 5 DECODING ASSESSMENT   **ADMINISTRATION**

SUBTEST A. SOUNDS   **GOAL 5/6**

D	a	s	ee	d	M

SUBTEST B. SMOOTH AND BUMPY BLENDING   **GOAL 2/2**

a m   am

SUBTEST C. SOUNDING OUT SMOOTHLY   **GOAL 4/4**

dad   me   add   seed

SUBTEST D. TRICKY WORDS   **GOAL 2/2**

said   I

SUBTEST E. SENTENCES   **GOAL 6/6**

I'm mad.

Dad said, "I see."

SCORING   If the student needs assistance the item is incorrect.
PASS   The student meets the goals on all subtest
NO PASS   The student fails to meet the goal on 1 or
             Review.

126   Blackline Master

STUDENT ASSESSMENT RECORD

Name _____ Jana _____

UNIT 5	ASSESSMENT ITEMS	SCORE/COMMENTS	
Subtest A	D a s ee d M	Goal 5/6 6 /6	
Subtest B	a·m am	Goal 2/2 2 /2	
Subtest C	d-ad dad me add seed	Goal 4/4 3 /4	Provide Extra Practice Lesson 1 Emphasize Smooth and Bumpy Blending with Dad. Practice throughout day and retest.
Subtest D	said I	Goal 2/2 2 /2	
Subtest E	I'm mad. Dad said, "I see."	Goal 6/6 6 /6	
Assessment Date(s): 9/23		Goals Met _4_ /5 Subtests P (all subtests) (NP)	

How to Administer Units 6–15

Units 6 through 8 continue assessing Smooth and Bumpy Blending. At Unit 9, this subtest is dropped. Beginning with Unit 6, each assessment includes a timing of the sentences.

While administering assessments, use each individual's Student Assessment Record to mark errors and record the number of seconds required to read the sentences. The following is a sample script for Unit 9.

Subtest A. Sounds

Have the student point to each item and say the sound.

Touch under the first sound. Read the sound. (/n/)

Read the next sound. (/W/)

Repeat with the remaining sounds.

Subtest B. Sounding Out Smoothly

Have the student do Smooth Blending of each word and then say the word.

I know you can read some of these words very quickly, but I want to see if you can still do Smooth Blending. So I'm going to have you *strrreeetch* each word out.

Put your finger under the first word and do Smooth Blending. (/Daaannn/)

Say the word. (Dan)

Repeat with the remaining words.

Subtest C. Tricky Words

Have the student identify each Tricky Word.

Put your finger under the first Tricky Word and read the word. (was)

Repeat with the remaining words.

Subtest D. Sentences

Have the student point to the first word and then read the sentence. Record the number of seconds needed to complete both sentences. (If a student hesitates on a word for three seconds, say the word and score as incorrect.)

You get to read sentences.

Put your finger under the first word and start when you're ready. (We see . . .)

General prescriptions are located at the bottom of each assessment.

Cho's Example

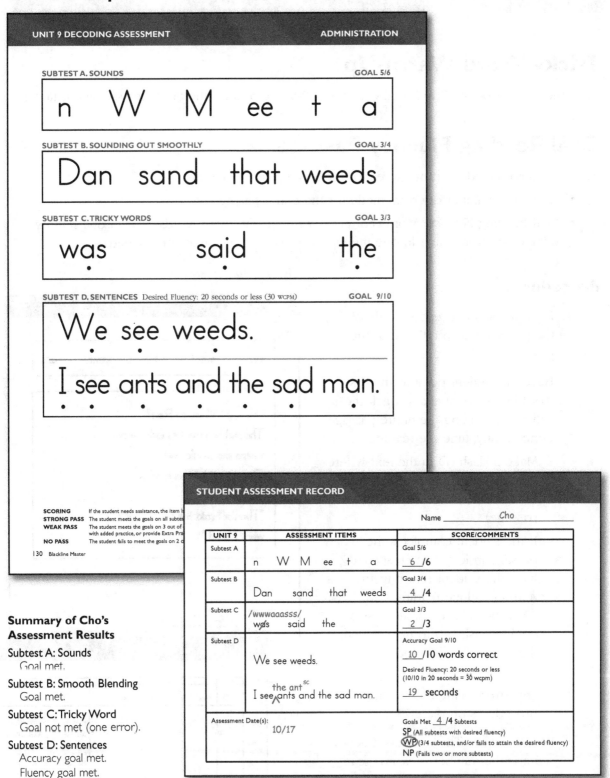

UNIT 9 DECODING ASSESSMENT ADMINISTRATION

SUBTEST A. SOUNDS GOAL 5/6

n   W   M   ee   t   a

SUBTEST B. SOUNDING OUT SMOOTHLY GOAL 3/4

Dan   sand   that   weeds

SUBTEST C. TRICKY WORDS GOAL 3/3

was   said   the

SUBTEST D. SENTENCES Desired Fluency: 20 seconds or less (30 WCPM) GOAL 9/10

We see weeds.

I see ants and the sad man.

SCORING If the student needs assistance, the item i...
STRONG PASS The student meets the goals on all subtes...
WEAK PASS The student meets the goals on 3 out of...
with added practice, or provide Extra Pra...
NO PASS The student fails to meet the goals on 2 o...

130 Blackline Master

STUDENT ASSESSMENT RECORD

Name _____ Cho _____

UNIT 9	ASSESSMENT ITEMS	SCORE/COMMENTS
Subtest A	n W M ee t a	Goal 5/6 __6__ /6
Subtest B	Dan sand that weeds	Goal 3/4 __4__ /4
Subtest C	/wwwaaasss/ waś said the	Goal 3/3 __2__ /3
Subtest D	We see weeds. the ant sc I see ˄ ants and the sad man.	Accuracy Goal 9/10 __10__ /10 words correct Desired Fluency: 20 seconds or less (10/10 in 20 seconds = 30 wcpm) __19__ seconds
Assessment Date(s): 10/17		Goals Met __4__ /4 Subtests SP (All subtests with desired fluency) (WP) (3/4 subtests, and/or fails to attain the desired fluency) NP (Fails two or more subtests)

Summary of Cho's Assessment Results

Subtest A: Sounds
Goal met.

Subtest B: Smooth Blending
Goal met.

Subtest C: Tricky Word
Goal not met (one error).

Subtest D: Sentences
Accuracy goal met.
Fluency goal met.

The student has a Weak Pass because she missed one Tricky Word. She is doing well with the blending process—even applying it to Tricky Words. The student should proceed forward with informal practice recognizing "was."

Oral Reading Fluency Assessments, Units 16–38

Tricky Word Warm-Up

Have the student point to and read each word. Mark errors on the Student Assessment Record.

Oral Reading Fluency Passage

Passing criteria include two measures for the *same* passage reading.

- Accuracy: Number of errors made for the entire passage
- Oral Reading Fluency: Words correct per minute (WCPM)—words read in one minute minus the errors made in one minute (a measure of accuracy and speed).

Procedures

1. Have the student read the title of the passage and predict what the passage will be about.

2. Have the student point to the first word in the passage and track the text while reading the entire passage. Concurrently, time the reading.

   - Make a slash (/) in the text where the student is at 60 seconds (but have the student complete the passage).

   - If the student completes the passage in less than 60 seconds, have the student return to the ★ and continue reading until 60 seconds have passed. Use a double slash (//) to mark where the student is at 60 seconds.

   - As the student reads, code any errors using the scoring procedures on page 73.

3. Record scores. The students' fluency score is the number of words read in 60 seconds minus the number of errors made during that minute. The accuracy score is the number of errors for the entire passage.

Tricky Word Warm-Up

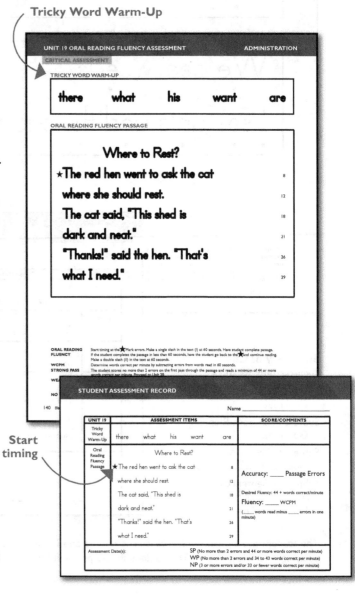

Start timing

Scoring

DIAGNOSTIC SCORING FOR UNITS 16–38	
If the student . . .	**Record . . .**
Needs Assistance Wait three seconds. Gently tell the student the correct response, draw a line through the item, and write an "A" for "assisted."	Incorrect *A* I hear the harsh wind.
Mispronounces a Word or Sound Draw a line through the item. Record what the student said.	Incorrect *shack* The cat said, "This shed is dark and neat."
Omits a Word or Word Part Circle the omission.	Incorrect The (red) hen went to ask the cat.
Inserts a Word Write what the student said, using a caret to show where the student inserted the word.	Incorrect *my* Mack said, "I should ask ^ Dad."
Self-Corrects If the student spontaneously self-corrects, write "SC" and score as a correct response.	Correct the sc Where is that nest?
If the student requires more than two attempts, score as an incorrect response.	Incorrect a/that/the It's in the tree.
Repeats Words Underline repeated words.	Correct Mack had to <u>think</u> hard.
Reverses Word Draw a line around the words as shown.	Correct "Sit still," said the man.

SECOND TIME THROUGH		
Any Error	Make a ✓ over each word.	✓ I left the park.

How to Administer Units 16–38

The following is a sample script for Unit 30.

Tricky Word Warm-Up

Have the student point to and read each word. Say something like:

Touch under the first Tricky Word. Read the word. **(They)**

Read the next word. **(of)**

Repeat with the remaining words.

Oral Reading Fluency Passage

Have the student point to each word and read the title. Say something like:

Read the title for me. **(The Farm)**

What do you think this story is going to be about?

Have the student point to each word and read the passage.

Start timing at the ★.

I'm going to have you read the story about the farm.

I'm going to time you, but I want you to read just like you always do.

Put your finger under the first word. You can start any time you are ready.

Record errors on the Student Assessment Record.

At 60 seconds, make a slash (/) in the text but have the student complete the passage. If the student completes the passage in less than 60 seconds, quickly point to the ★ and say something like:

Wow! Keep reading until I say stop.

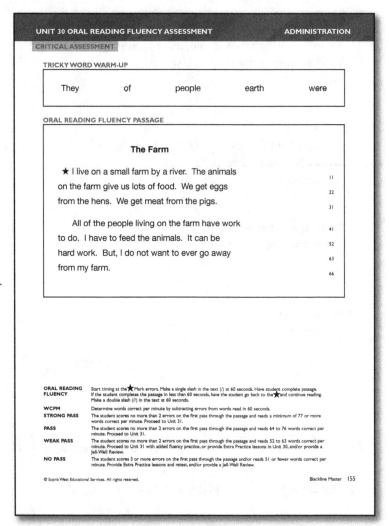

UNIT 30 ORAL READING FLUENCY ASSESSMENT | ADMINISTRATION

CRITICAL ASSESSMENT

TRICKY WORD WARM-UP

They	of	people	earth	were

ORAL READING FLUENCY PASSAGE

The Farm

★ I live on a small farm by a river. The animals
on the farm give us lots of food. We get eggs
from the hens. We get meat from the pigs.

   All of the people living on the farm have work
to do. I have to feed the animals. It can be
hard work. But, I do not want to ever go away
from my farm.

11
22
31
41
52
63
66

ORAL READING FLUENCY — Start timing at the ★. Mark errors. Make a single slash in the text (/) at 60 seconds. Have student complete passage. If the student completes the passage in less than 60 seconds, have the student go back to the ★ and continue reading. Make a double slash (//) in the text at 60 seconds.

WCPM — Determine words correct per minute by subtracting errors from words read in 60 seconds.

STRONG PASS — The student scores no more than 2 errors on the first pass through the passage and reads a minimum of 77 or more words correct per minute. Proceed to Unit 31.

PASS — The student scores no more than 2 errors on the first pass through the passage and reads 64 to 76 words correct per minute. Proceed to Unit 31.

WEAK PASS — The student scores no more than 2 errors on the first pass through the passage and reads 52 to 63 words correct per minute. Proceed to Unit 31 with added fluency practice, or provide Extra Practice lessons in Unit 30, and/or provide a Jell-Well Review.

NO PASS — The student scores 3 or more errors on the first pass through the passage and/or reads 51 or fewer words correct per minute. Provide Extra Practice lessons and retest, and/or provide a Jell-Well Review.

Blackline Master 155

Michael and Hannah's Example

STUDENT ASSESSMENT RECORD

Name ___Michael A.___

UNIT 30	ASSESSMENT ITEMS		SCORE/COMMENTS
Tricky Word Warm-Up	They of people earth	where ~~were~~	Practice "were" and "where"
Oral Reading Fluency Passage	**The Farm**		**Accuracy:** _2_
	★ I live on a small farm by a river. A^{sc} The animals	11	**Passage Errors**
	on the farm give us lots of food. We get eggs	22	
	from the hens. We get meat from the pigs.	31	Desired Fluency: 77+ words correct/minute
	All of the people living on the farm ~~have~~ had work	41	
	to do. I have to feed the animals. It can be	52	**Fluency:** _58_ WCPM
	hard work. But, I do not want/to ever go away	63	(_59_ words read minus
	the from my farm. 60 seconds	66	_1_ errors in one minute)

Assessment Date(s): 11/21

SP (No more than 2 errors and 77 or more words correct per minute)
P (No more than 2 errors and 64 to 76 words correct per minute)
(WP) (No more than 2 errors and 52 to 63 words correct per minute)
NP (3 or more errors and/or 51 or fewer words correct per minute)

STUDENT ASSESSMENT RECORD

Name ___Hannah___

UNIT 30	ASSESSMENT ITEMS		SCORE/COMMENTS
Tricky Word Warm-Up	They of people earth were		No errors
Oral Reading Fluency Passage	**The Farm**		**Accuracy:** _2_
	★ I live on a (small) farm by a river. The animals	11	**Passage Errors**
	on the farm give us lots of food. We get eggs	22	
	✓ from the hens. We get meat from the pigs.	31	Desired Fluency: 77+ words correct/minute
	All of the/people living on the farm have work	41	
	to do. I have to feed the animals. It can be	52	**Fluency:** _97_ WCPM
	hard work. But, I do not want to ever go away	63	(_100_ words read minus
	the from my farm.	66	_3_ errors in one minute)

Assessment Date(s): 11/16

(SP) (No more than 2 errors and 77 or more words correct per minute)
P (No more than 2 errors and 64 to 76 words correct per minute)
WP (No more than 2 errors and 52 to 63 words correct per minute)
NP (3 or more errors and/or 51 or fewer words correct per minute)

Decoding Diagnoses, Selected Units 19-38

By Unit 16, the assessments are no longer diagnostic. Instead, the global oral reading fluency score is used to assess progress. If students have difficulty passing the assessments, the Decoding Diagnosis can be used to more accurately diagnose specific problems. A Decoding Diagnosis is included for Units 19, 23, 26, 28, 30, 34, 36, and 38.

How to Administer a Decoding Diagnosis

1. Have the student read from the Decoding Diagnosis. Score on a separate copy.

2. For each subtest, have the student point to and read each item.

3. Make a slash through any item the student misses and record what the student said above the missed item.

UNIT 19 DECODING DIAGNOSIS   **ADMINISTRATION**

SOUNDS

ĕ	Th	r	k	oo	E	ar	wh
i	sh	ee	Wh	a	ĕ	H	ea

VOWEL DISCRIMINATION

~~set~~ *sit*	sat	sit	seat
Mark	Mick	M~~ack~~ *Mark*	m~~ee~~k *meet*

BEGINNING QUICK SOUNDS

d~~ent~~ *dash*	hand	t~~est~~ *rest*	dark
hit	tent	Kim	dash

BLENDS AND WORD ENDINGS

Trish *Tr-ish*	sn~~ack~~ *smack*	creek	kitten
scoot	wham	drink	scat

TRICKY WORDS

where	into	as	wouldn't
what	to	There	are

• Have students read from a clean copy of the Decoding Diagnosis. Record incorrect responses on another copy.
• Use information from both the Unit 19 Decoding Assessment and the Unit 19 Decoding Diagnosis to identify specific skill deficits.

Blackline Master 141

NOTE
In this example, the student had difficulty passing Unit 19 Assessment. The teacher administered the Decoding Diagnosis and determined the student is firm on sounds but is not systematically applying them in word reading. See page 103 for prescriptions.

SECTION 4

Making Decisions

This section explains how to adjust instruction to meet the changing needs of your students. Each segment provides information tailored to the developmental progress of students.

Every *Read Well* teacher is a diagnostician.

Adjusting Instruction

Many factors may affect students' progress—a sudden insight into the process of blending, absences, attention span, and so on. Assessment results will help you adjust instruction and practice to meet the changing needs of your groups and of individual children. Meet with your colleagues frequently to adjust groups.

Options for Adjusting Instruction

Read Well assessment results assist you in determining when to:

- Accelerate groups and/or individuals
- Develop interventions for groups and/or individuals

Analyzing Scores

Copy assessment scores from students' Assessment Records to the Group Assessment Record. (As subtests vary across units, several different forms are provided for your convenience. Blackline masters of the Group Assessment Records are on pages 192–198 of this manual.)

The Group Assessment Record allows you to:

- Analyze the strengths and weaknesses of a group of students
- Compare the progress of individual students with the group
- Quickly share assessment results with colleagues
- Make regrouping decisions

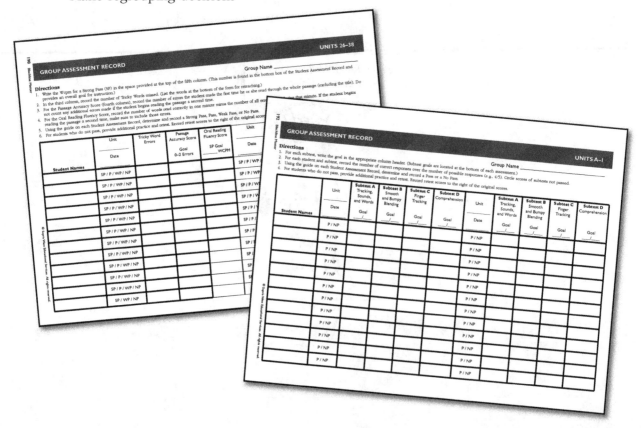

At the end of each unit, review your Group Assessment Record. If you are part of a walk-to-read program, meet on a regular basis to share results, problem-solve, and regroup as appropriate.

GENERAL PRESCRIPTIONS		
Who	**Score**	**Then . . .**
An entire small group	Strong Pass	Continue forward. Consider a faster pace of instruction.
Part of a small group Individuals		Consider regrouping for acceleration.
An entire small group	Pass	Continue forward at the same pace of instruction.
Part of a small group Individuals		Consider regrouping. (See prescriptions for students with Weak and No Passes.)
An entire small group	Weak Pass	Practice a difficult skill throughout the day with the whole class. Emphasize instruction and practice on any difficult skills while: • Providing Extra Practice lessons for the unit • Reteaching lessons or the unit
Part of a small group Individuals		Consider regrouping. Provide a second dose of instruction for these students. Emphasize instruction and practice on any difficult skills while: • Providing Extra Practice lessons for the unit • Reteaching lessons or the unit • Previewing the next unit
An entire small group	No Pass	Consider regrouping. Provide a second dose of instruction for these students. Emphasize instruction and practice on any difficult skills while: • Providing Extra Practice lessons for the unit
Part of a small group		• Reteaching lessons or the unit • Previewing the next unit
Individuals		• Providing a Jell Woll Review of previous units (see Section 5)

STRONG PASS/PASS

Most students will receive Strong Passes and Passes when placed appropriately, grouped appropriately, given sufficient instructional time, and taught well.

Double Dosing

Read Well's flexible construction makes it possible to help children become independent readers at an optimum rate. Schools often give some children a double dose of *Read Well* instruction to maximize progress.

A double dose of *Read Well* instruction may be provided:

FOR	BY	WHEN	WITH
• A group • Part of a group • An individual student	• Another teacher (classroom or specialist) • Paraprofessional • Parent volunteer • Older student • Peer	• Before school • After school • During school	• Additional *Read Well* lessons within a day • Extra practice within a unit • Preteaching lessons • Reteaching lessons • Remediation of a skill • Jell-Well Review (recycling)

Note: In some cases, schools intervene aggressively with a triple dose of *Read Well* instruction and practice for the highest risk students.

Using Assessment Results, Units A and B

Units A and B are intervention units that provide direct instruction in basic readiness skills—one-to-one correspondence between a symbol and a word, tracking, recognition of common school objects, learning what a sound is, phonemic awareness, and identifying who a story is about.

Pass/No Pass

At the bottom of each assessment, you will find the criteria for a Pass or No Pass and general instructions for what to do next.

SAMPLE: UNIT A	
Pass	The student meets the goal on all subtests. Proceed to Unit B.
No Pass	The student fails to meet the goal on one or more subtests. Provide Extra Practice lessons and seek peer consultation. Consider providing instruction in *Read Well K*, Preludes A through F.

Intervention Flow Chart

Students who require intervention to pass Units A and B may need additional instruction as they proceed through *Read Well 1*. The flow chart demonstrates how to provide ongoing intervention using assessment results and *Read Well 1* Extra Practice or *Read Well K* units for intervention.

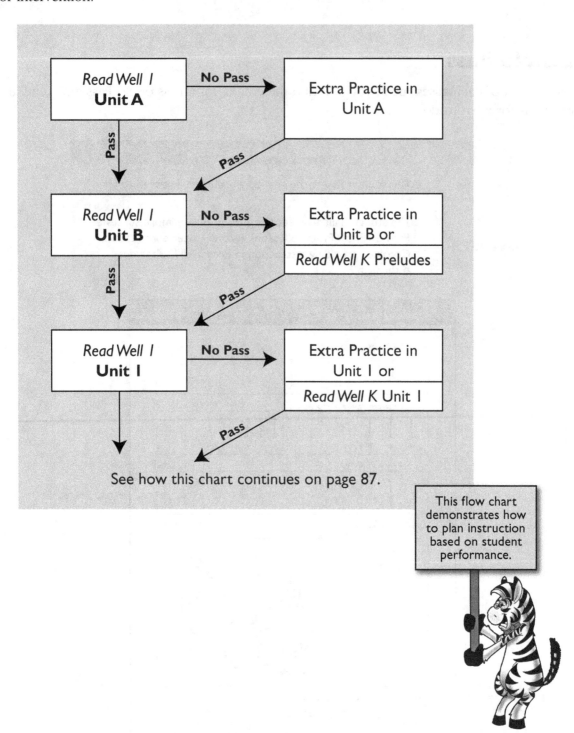

| *Read Well 1* **Unit A** | — No Pass → | Extra Practice in Unit A |

Pass ↓ ↙ *Pass*

| *Read Well 1* **Unit B** | — No Pass → | Extra Practice in Unit B or *Read Well K* Preludes |

Pass ↓ ↙ *Pass*

| *Read Well 1* **Unit 1** | — No Pass → | Extra Practice in Unit 1 or *Read Well K* Unit 1 |

↓ ↙ *Pass*

See how this chart continues on page 87.

This flow chart demonstrates how to plan instruction based on student performance.

Diagnostic-Prescriptive Teaching

When students have difficulty, diagnose or pinpoint error patterns. Provide an increased instructional focus on the weak skills while maintaining a balanced daily lesson. Examples follow.

SPECIFIC PRESCRIPTIONS FOR UNITS A AND B	
If students have difficulty with . . .	**Then try these prescriptions . . .**
Finger Tracking	• Use Finger Tracking Games such as Simon Says. • Motivate young children to track text with little gimmicks such as witch fingers placed on the fingers of those who track text. • Pay more attention to students who are tracking than those who are not—"Martha gets a turn all by herself because she is doing Finger Tracking." • Seat children so that you can guide the hands of those most in need of assistance.
Smooth Blending	Have the whole class practice phonemic awareness skills informally throughout the day using: • Stretch and Shrink with names • Smooth and Bumpy Blending with "I" • Stretch and Shrink games: How long can you stretch out "I"? Ensure that the adults teaching this skill can do Stretch and Shrink without stopping between sounds. Practice as needed. Work with individuals on Stretch and Shrink and Sound Counting. Demonstrate, guide, and have the student practice independent of your voice. *(continued)*

SPECIFIC PRESCRIPTIONS FOR UNITS A AND B (*continued*)	
If students have difficulty with . . .	**Then try these prescriptions . . .**
Sound and Word Recognition	• Write the word or sound on a card. • Tape the card on the child's desk with a sticky note covering it. Ham it up! Have the classroom teacher, paraprofessional, and volunteers working in the room ask the student to peek under the sticky note throughout the day and tell what the secret sound or word is. Say something like: Let's look under your sticky note. What's your secret sound? Later in the day, say: Oh dear! I've forgotten what your secret sound is. Let's look at it. What's your secret sound?
Comprehension	Have a volunteer work with one or two students each day if they have difficulty identifying who the story is about in Subtest D. Have the volunteer read a short picture book to the student or students, frequently asking "Who is the story about?" Once students can identify who a story is about with different books, have the volunteer add the following prompt: "What does [character's name] want?" and "What happened at the end?" Eventually, questions about the sequence of events or action can be added.

DISTRIBUTE PRACTICE

Frequent practice within a day and across days can help students develop the depth of knowledge required for long-term retention.

Washington School Example—First Grade, Group 8

Group 8 is composed of four first grade students. Three of the four students have transferred from other schools. Placement Inventory scores were as follows:

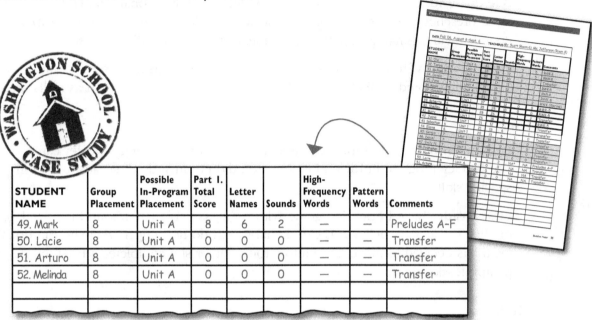

STUDENT NAME	Group Placement	Possible In-Program Placement	Part I. Total Score	Letter Names	Sounds	High-Frequency Words	Pattern Words	Comments
49. Mark	8	Unit A	8	6	2	—	—	Preludes A–F
50. Lacie	8	Unit A	0	0	0	—	—	Transfer
51. Arturo	8	Unit A	0	0	0	—	—	Transfer
52. Melinda	8	Unit A	0	0	0	—	—	Transfer

Students have completed 6-Day Plans in Units A and B. The results of assessments for A and B are shown below.

GROUP ASSESSMENT RECORD UNITS A–1

Directions
1. For each subtest, record the goal in the column header. (Subtest goals are located on each assessment.)
2. For each student, record the number of correct responses over the number of possible responses on each subtest. Circle scores for subtests not passed.
3. If a student meets goals on 4 of the 4 subtests, circle P (Pass). If a student fails to meet goals on 1 or more subtests, circle NP (No Pass).
4. If a student scores a No Pass, seek consultation. Provide additional practice and retest. Record retest scores to the right of the original score.

Group Name ___Group 8___

Student Names	Unit A Date	Subtest A Tracking, Sounds, and Words Goal 5/5	Subtest B Smooth and Bumpy Blending Goal 2/2	Subtest C Sentences Goal 3/3	Subtest D Comprehension Goal 1/1	Unit B Date	Subtest A Tracking, Sounds, and Words Goal 5/5	Subtest B Smooth and Bumpy Blending Goal 4/4	Subtest C Sentences Goal 3/3	Subtest D Comprehension Goal 1/1
Mark	Ⓟ/NP	5/5	2/2	3/3	1/1	Ⓟ/NP	5/5	4/4	3/3	1/1
Lacie	Ⓟ/NP	5/5	2/2	3/3	1/1	Ⓟ/NP	5/5	4/4	3/3	1/1
Arturo	Ⓟ/NP	5/5	2/2	3/3	1/1	P/ⓃⓅ	5/5	③/4	3/3	⓪/1
Melinda	P/ⓃⓅ	5/5	①/2 2/2	3/3	⓪/1 1/1	Ⓟ/NP	5/5	4/4	3/3	1/1
	P/NP					P/NP				
	P/NP					P/NP				
	P/NP					P/NP				
	P/NP					P/NP				
	P/NP					P/NP				
	P/NP					P/NP				
	P/NP					P/NP				
	P/NP					P/NP				

Prescriptions For Group 8

Mark

Background: Mark has been on an Individualized Educational Plan (IEP) since preschool. During kindergarten, he worked slowly through the *Read Well K* Preludes with a small group of three students and individualized assistance.

First Grade: With the preludes as a foundation, Mark was able to pass Units A and B. Mr. Matthews predicts that Mark will need more intensive instruction as skills progress.

Lacie

Background: Lacie is a transfer student. She is currently living in foster care. The literacy program in Lacie's kindergarten did not include direct instruction in specific skills.

First Grade: Lacie began first grade with no measurable letter/sound knowledge, but the first grade team believes Lacie's initial scores do not reflect what she can do. The team has decided to move Lacie into Group 7 after she completes a brief tutorial with a paraprofessional.

Melinda

Background: Melinda is a transfer student with articulation problems and language delays. No records have been forwarded to the school.

First Grade: Melinda is the only student who was unable to pass the Unit A Assessment. After Melinda had difficulty with the assessment, Mr. Matthews began providing 10-minute tutorials with her during the one-hour reading block. The team believes that with intensive one-to-one instruction, Melinda will be able to pass Units A and B.

Arturo

Background: Arturo is a transfer student and an English Language Learner.

Intervention: Arturo passed Unit A easily, but had difficulty blending "I'm" in Unit B and answering a comprehension question. Mr. Matthews has conferred with the ELL teacher, who will begin preteaching portions of the lessons with a focus on blending, language, and comprehension.

Projected Schedule for Mark, Lacie, Melinda, and Arturo

Mr. Matthews anticipates that Mark, Arturo, and Melinda will require intensive instruction and practice through the year. He will use both *Read Well 1* and *Read Well K* to extend practice. When Lacie has been successfully moved to Group 7, Mark, Arturo, and Melinda will receive a second daily dose of *Read Well* instruction with the paraprofessional.

Using Assessment Results, Units 1–5

Units 1–5 create a foundation of learning for later units. Mastery in the early units is critical for success in the remaining units.

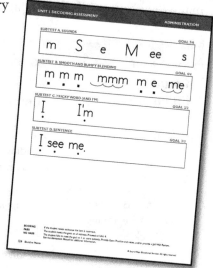

Pass/No Pass

At the bottom of each assessment for Units 1–5, you will find the criteria for a Pass or No Pass. The criteria remain high through the early units.

SAMPLE: UNIT 3	
Pass	The student meets the goals on all subtests. Proceed to Unit 4.
No Pass	The student fails to meet the goals on 1 or more subtests. Provide Extra Practice lessons and retest and/or provide a Jell-Well Review.

This flow chart demonstrates how to plan instruction based on student performance.

JELL-WELL REVIEW

If students score a No Pass on two consecutive units, consider a quick review of previous units. See Section 5.

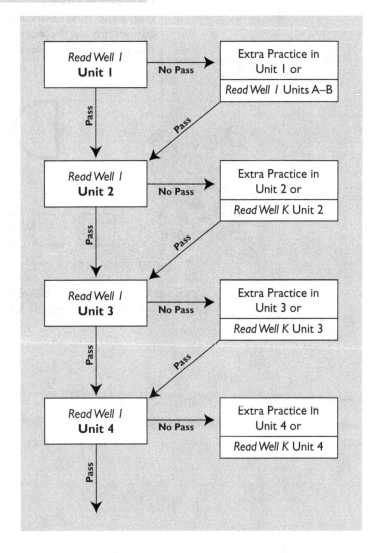

Diagnostic-Prescriptive Teaching

If students have difficulty with a specific skill, focus instruction on weak skills while maintaining practice on all skills. Examples follow.

SPECIFIC PRESCRIPTIONS FOR UNITS 1–5	
If students have difficulty with . . .	**Then try these prescriptions . . .**
Smooth Blending	Seek peer consultation if all students do not pass Subtest B, Smooth and Bumpy Blending, in Unit 2. You may find that you have been stopping between sounds as you model. If so, work with a colleague and reteach.
Smooth Blending With a Beginning Quick Sound	• Provide Extra Practice Lesson 1 with additional practice blending /d/. • Provide repeated practice with the Smooth and Bumpy Blending Card #12. • Give each student in the group a special practice card.

PRACTICE CARD

I can blend "Dad" smoothly. Listen to me really *ssstrrreeetch* out the word, without pausing between the sounds. When I do this, please initial one of the boxes.

Dad

☐ ☐ ☐ ☐ ☐

If students rapidly master the difficult skill, reassess as soon as possible. A day or two of intense practice may be sufficient to master a difficult skill.

SPECIFIC PRESCRIPTIONS FOR UNITS 1–5 (continued)	
If students have difficulty with . . .	**Then try these prescriptions . . .**
Smooth Blending Beginning Quick Sound /D/	Have the whole class practice blending "dad" throughout the day and across days. Provide practice with: • Stretch and Shrink with /daaad/ • dad • Smooth and Bumpy Blending with "dad" • Dictation on white boards with "dad," "sad," and "mad"
Tricky Word Recognition	• Write the word or sound on the child's hand with a washable marker. • Have the student read his or her special word to others throughout the day and use the word in a sentence. Say something like: Show me your special word. What's your word? (said) What did Mrs. Jones say? (It's time for recess.) Say, "Mrs. Jones said, 'It's time for recess.'" (Mrs. Jones said, "It's time for recess.")

Washington School Example—First Grade, Group 7

All four students in Group 7 are transfer students.

Prescriptions For Group 7

GROUP ASSESSMENT RECORD — **UNITS 2–4**

Directions
1. For each subtest, record the goal in the column header. (Subtest goals are located on each assessment.) Group Name ___Group 7___
2. For each student, record the number of correct responses over the number of possible responses on each subtest. Circle scores for subtests not passed.
3. If a student meets goals on 4 of the 4 subtests, circle P (Pass). If a student fails to meet goals on 1 or more subtests, circle NP (No Pass).
4. If a student scores a No Pass, seek consultation. Provide additional practice and retest. Record retest scores to the right of the original score.

Student Names	Unit 3 Date	Subtest A Sounds Goal 5/6	Subtest B Smooth and Bumpy Blending Goal 4/4	Subtest C Tricky Words Goal 2/2	Subtest D Sentences Goal 3/3	Unit 4 Date	Subtest A Sounds Goal 5/6	Subtest B Smooth and Bumpy Blending Goal 3/4	Subtest C Tricky Words Goal 2/2	Subtest D Sentences Goal 5/5
Sergio	(P) NP	6/6	4/4	2/2	3/3	(P) NP	6/6	4/4	2/2	5/5
Daniel	(P) NP	6/6	4/4	2/2	3/3	(P) NP	6/6	4/4	2/2	5/5
Emily N.	(P) NP	6/6	4/4	2/2	3/3	(P)(NP)	6/6	4/4	2/2	5/5
Christopher*	P (NP)	5/6	(2/4)(2/4) (1/2) 2/2 (2/3) 3/3			P (NP)	5/6	(2/4)(2/4) (1/2) 2/2		(3/5)(3/5)
	P / NP					P / NP				
	P / NP									
	P / NP									

> Use good judgement. If a student with sinus problems has difficulty blending /mmmeee/ smoothly, but has mastered all other skills, pass the student to the next unit. Watch progress carefully.

Sergio, Daniel, Emily

Background: Sergio, Daniel, and Emily have all transferred in from other kindergarten programs. Little is known about their previous literacy preparation.

First Grade: Because students have had Units 1 and 2 in whole class instruction, Ms. Jefferson follows the 2-Day Plan for Units 1 and 2, a 3-Day Plan for Unit 3, and a 4-Day Plan for Unit 4. (Unit 4 introduces a new vowel.) Sergio, Daniel, and Emily pass all assessments easily.

Christopher

Background: Christopher is a transfer student as well. He has frequent colds and is often absent from school. When in school, Christopher has difficulty paying attention.

First Grade: During the first two units, Christopher has some difficulty keeping up. Though he passes assessments, Ms. Jefferson notices that Christopher's response rate is slower than others in his group. Christopher is also unable to sustain /mmm/ because of his sinus difficulties and has a hard time with Stretch and Shrink (phonemic awareness activities).

Intervention and Regrouping: Ms. Jefferson has her paraprofessional work with Christopher in a tutorial from five to ten minutes each day. However, by Unit 4, Christopher is barely holding his own and will keep the group from moving forward. At the first team meeting, the staff decides that Christopher will move to Group 8.

Using Assessment Results, Units 6–15

Units 6–15 strengthen and build on the skills learned in Units 1–5. In Unit 6, a desired fluency goal is added to the subtest on sentence reading.

Note: The goal of instruction in Units 6–15 is not speed. The goal is accuracy and mastery of blending. However, the added fluency measure objectively assesses students developing skills. Students who are not able to meet the desired fluency goals need more intensive practice.

Strong Pass, Weak Pass, No Pass

At the bottom of each assessment for Units 6–15, you will find the criteria for a Strong Pass, a Weak Pass, and a No Pass.

SAMPLE: UNIT 10	
Strong Pass	The student meets the goals on all subtests and has attained the desired fluency. Proceed to Unit 11.
Weak Pass	The student meets the goals on 3 out of 4 subtests, and/or fails to attain the desired fluency. Proceed to Unit 11 with added practice, or provide Extra Practice lessons in Unit 10, and/or provide a Jell-Well Review.
No Pass	The student fails to meet the goals on 2 or more subtests. Provide Extra Practice lessons and retest and/or provide a Jell-Well Review.

In Units A–5, the sample Pass/No Pass system provided sufficient information to ensure that a strong foundation was being established. The new Strong Pass/Weak Pass/No Pass system in these units provides additional instructional options.

- Consistent Strong Passes signal the possibility of moving faster.

- A Weak Pass indicates the need for additional work to achieve mastery.

  Weak Passes for two consecutive units are an indication that future difficulties are likely without intervention. With repeated Weak Passes, the student's burden of learning will eventually become overwhelming. A Weak Pass is a red flag.

- A No Pass indicates the need for immediate intervention.

Intervention

Early intervention is strongly recommended as it serves as a basis for later learning. Time spent on building mastery in the early units will result in faster mastery in later units and will prevent students from becoming overwhelmed.

Intervention Flow Chart

This flow chart demonstrates how to plan instruction based on student performance.

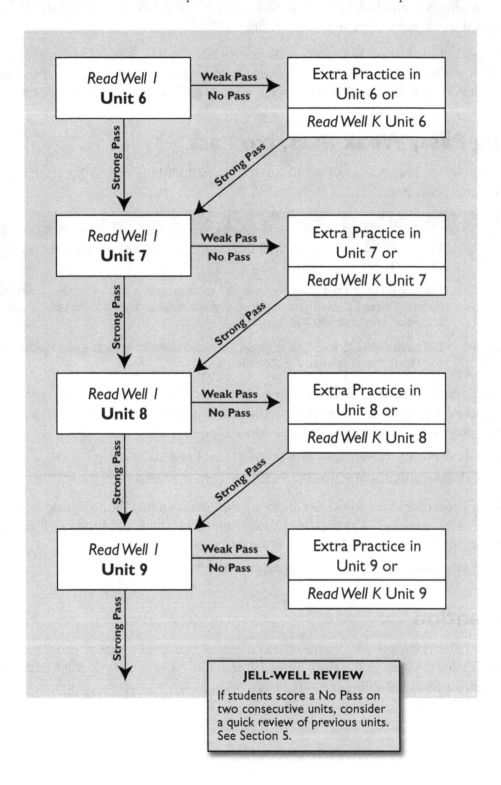

Diagnostic-Prescriptive Teaching

Continue to diagnose or pinpoint error patterns. Examples of prescriptions for implementation with groups or individuals follow.

SPECIFIC PRESCRIPTIONS FOR UNITS 6–15	
If students have difficulty with . . .	**Then try these prescriptions . . .**
A Sound (/iii/)	a. During Sound Card practice, add four more cards with the small letter i. Each time i comes up, have students stop and think before responding. Provide descriptive feedback, referring to the key word for /iii/. Say something like: Let's see if you can get the hard sound /iii/ four times. You got the hard sound—/iii/ as in insect—once. You got the hard sound—/iii/ as in insect—twice. You got the hard sound—/iii/ as in insect—three times. You got the hard sound—/iii/ as in insect—four times! b. During Decoding Practice, have students see who can sustain the sound /iii/ the longest. c. During Accuracy and Fluency practice, have students read the sound twice in rhythm and then read the word. /i/, /i/, in /i/, /i/, tin /i/, /i/, win d. If students have difficulty with /i/, place a card on each child's desk with the letter i and a picture of insects. Make six spaces on the card for someone to initial. • Assign each student with a study buddy who sits nearby. • Teach the study buddy to say: Tell me your special sound and word. (/i/ as in "insect") • Teach the study buddy to assist if needed, compliment the child, and initial the card. • When the card is completed, provide each child with something to acknowledge his or her efforts.
Sounding Out Smoothly	• Using the same words, precede Sounding Out Smoothly with Stretch and Shrink. • Provide additional practice with Smooth and Bumpy Blending. (Make new cards for any difficult words.) • Have students identify whether you are doing Smooth or Bumpy Blending. • Work briefly with individuals, demonstrating, guiding practice, and providing individual turns.

SPECIFIC PRESCRIPTIONS FOR UNITS 6–15 *(continued)*	
If students have difficulty with . . .	**Then try these prescriptions . . .**

Tricky Words
 	
(would, could, should)

	Practice orally spelling one or two difficult Tricky Words or a Tricky Word pattern.
	
	• Day 1: Write "would," "could," and "should" on the board. Have the class orally spell the words in the morning, before lunch, after lunch, and before going home.
	
	• Day 2: Erase the <u>c</u>, <u>w</u>, and <u>sh</u> from each word, replacing the letters with dashes (e.g., –ould). Have the class orally spell the words in the morning, before lunch, after lunch, and before going home.
	
	• Day 3: Write each word on a card. Have students who know the words dictate the words from the cards. Have the class orally spell the words. Say something like:
	
	    [Charlie], please dictate the first word. **(would)**
	    I *would* like to eat soon. [Charlie], say the word. **(would)**
	    Everyone, spell "would." **(<u>w-o-u-l-d</u>)**
	
	    [Yun], please dictate the next word. **(could)**
	    I *could* read the book. [Yun], say the word. **(could)**
	    Everyone, spell "could." **(<u>c-o-u-l-d</u>)**
	
	    [Ruth], please dictate the next word. **(should)**
	    I *should* do my best.
	    [Ruth], say the word. **(should)**
	    Everyone, spell "should." **(<u>s-h-o-u-l-d</u>)**
	
	• Day 4: Erase "-ould" from the board. Have students who have had difficulty assist you with dictation. Have the class orally spell the words.
	
	• Day 5: Have students who have had difficulty assist you with dictation. Have the class write the words on paper or on white boards.

Fluency	a. Begin each day's lesson with five minutes of sustained independent practice.
	  • Provide each student with a notebook or booklet of *Read Well* Homework Stories.
	  • Have each student point to the words and whisper read for five minutes. Students should begin with Unit 2 and read stories consecutively.
	  • Each child's goal is to read a little more each day. Each child can mark where he or she is at the end of five minutes with a sticky note.
	
	b. Begin each day's story reading with a review of the previous day's story.
	
	c. Select paragraphs from review stories for Short Passage Practice. Demonstrate expressive reading. Guide reading. Have individuals read the passage.
	
	d. Review homework procedures. A grade-level routine and full implementation of recommended procedures can result in nearly 100% success with homework completion.

Washington School Example— Second Grade, Remedial Group

The following group is composed of eight students who have transferred into Washington School as second graders. At the beginning of the school year, students placed in *Read Well 1* Unit 5. Students knew 26 out of 26 letter names, most of the consonant sounds, and some sight words. None of the children had blending skills.

As second grade students, the children are already a year below grade level.

GROUP ASSESSMENT RECORD   **UNITS 9–15**

Directions
1. For each subtest, record the goal in the column header. (Subtest goals are located on each assessment.)
2. For each student, record the number of correct responses over the number of possible responses on each subtest. Circle scores for subtests not passed.
3. For the last column of eachc unit, record the number of seconds to completion during Sentence Reading. Circle scores that do not reach the Desired Fluency Goal.
4. If a student meets goals on 5 of the 5 subtests, and has attained the desired fluency, circle SP (Strong Pass). If a student meets goals on 4 of the 5 subtests and/or fails to attain the desired fluency, circle WP (Weak Pass). If a student fails to meet goals on 2 or more subtests, circle NP (No Pass).
5. If a student scores a No Pass, provide additional practice and retest. Record retest scores to the right of the original score.

Group Name _____ Mrs. Wong, 2nd grade

Student Names	Unit 11 Date	Subtest A Sounds Goal 6 / 7	Subtest B Sounding Out Smoothly Goal 4 / 5	Subtest C Tricky Words Goal 3 / 4	Subtest D Sentences Goal 13 / 15	Sentence Fluency Desired Fluency Goal 30 secs.	Unit 12 Date	Subtest A Sounds Goal 6 / 7	Subtest B Sounding Out Smoothly Goal 4 / 5	Subtest C Tricky Words Goal 3 / 4	Subtest D Sentences Goal 14 / 16	Sentence Fluency Desired Fluency Goal 30 secs.
Maya	SP /(WP)/ NP	6/7	4/5	3/4	(12/15)	(31)	SP (WP)/ NP	7/7	4/5	3/4	15/16	(33)
Nick	SP /(WP)/ NP	6/7	4/5	3/4	13/15	(32)	SP (WP)/ NP	7/7	4/5	3/4	14/16	(32)
Ruben	(SP)/ WP / NP	7/7	4/5	4/4	14/15	25	(SP)/ WP / NP	7/7	4/5	3/4	16/16	24
Brittany	(SP)/ WP / NP	7/7	5/5	3/4	14/15	24	(SP)/ WP / NP	7/7	5/5	4/4	16/16	23
Beatrice	(SP)/ WP / NP	7/7	4/5	4/4	15/15	25	(SP)/ WP / NP	6/7	4/5	3/4	16/16	25
Daniel	(SP)/ WP / NP	7/7	5/5	4/4	15/15	26	(SP)/ WP / NP	7/7	5/5	4/4	16/16	24
Lacey	(SP)/ WP / NP	6/7	5/5	4/4	14/15	26	(SP)/ WP / NP	7/7	5/5	3/4	15/16	24
Emilio	(SP)/ WP / NP	7/7	5/5	3/4	13/15	23	(SP)/ WP / NP	7/7	5/5	3/4	15/16	25
	SP / WP / NP						SP / WP / NP					
	SP / WP / NP						SP / WP / NP					
	SP / WP / NP						SP / WP / NP					

The desired fluency should be 30 seconds or less for this unit. Lower numbers are better.

Prescriptions For Second Grade, Remedial Group

Second Grade Schedule

This group of students receives a double dose of *Read Well* instruction each day—a one-hour reading block in the morning with the second grade team and an additional half hour in the afternoon with the Title 1 teacher. Units 6–10 were each completed in three days with the two teachers collaboratively following a 6-Day Plan.

- The morning block teacher completed the plans for Days 1, 3, and 5.

- The afternoon teacher completed the plans for Days 2, 4, and 6.

6-DAY PLAN • Pre-Intervention		
Day 1 • Decoding Practice 1 • Introduction and Story 1 • Skill Work 1*	**Day 2** • Review Decoding Practice 1 • Story 2 • Comprehension Work 2* • Homework 1, Story 2*	**Day 3** • Decoding Practice 2 • Story 3 • Skill Work 3*
Day 4 • Review Decoding Practice 2 • Story 4 • Comprehension Work 4* • Homework 2, Story 4*	**Day 5** • Decoding Practice 3 • Story 5 and Story Summary • Skill Work 5* • Homework 4, Storybook Decoding Review*	**Day 6** • Decoding Practice 4 • Story 6 (Student Summary) • Skill Work 6* • Homework 3, Story 6*

By Unit 11, Maya and Nick are beginning to have difficulty, as noted by their fluency scores in Units 11 and 12. (See previous page.)

Maya and Nick • A Triple Dose

Rather than slow down the progress of the group, the teachers decide to provide Maya and Nick with additional practice, ten minutes each day with a review Solo Story.

- The children are provided with tutors from the fifth grade two days per week, help from AmeriCorp volunteers two days per week, and a special session with the principal on Fridays.

- Tutors are trained to begin each session by listening to their student read a different story each day, using the charting and timing procedures on Extra Practice Activity 2.

- When the child has completed the Extra Practice Activity, the reading is recorded.

- Each session then begins by having the student listen to his or her recorded story from the day before.

- The last recording of each week can be shared with the principal as an informal but very special celebration.

By Unit 15, Maya and Nick score Strong Passes on their assessments. The students continue working with the fifth grade tutors two days per week and continue sharing their accomplishments with the principal. By Unit 25, Nick and Maya begin tutoring two first grade students who have transferred into Washington School.

Using Assessment Results, Units 16–38

Units 16–38 strengthen and build on the skills learned in Units 1–15. In Unit 16, assessments shift from diagnostic Decoding Assessments to Oral Reading Fluency Assessments.

Strong Pass, Pass, Weak Pass, No Pass

At the bottom of each assessment, you will find the criteria for a Strong Pass, Weak Pass, and a No Pass. Criteria for a Pass is added at Unit 26.

SAMPLE: UNIT 26	
Strong Pass	The student scores no more than 2 errors on the first pass through the passage and reads a minimum of 65 or more words correct per minute. Proceed to Unit 27.
Pass	The student scores no more than 2 errors on the first pass through the passage and reads 56 to 64 words correct per minute. Proceed to Unit 27.
Weak Pass	The student scores no more than 2 errors on the first pass through the passage and reads 48 to 55 words correct per minute. Proceed to Unit 27 with added fluency practice, or provide Extra Practice lessons in Unit 26, and/or provide a Jell-Well Review.
No Pass	The student scores 3 or more errors on the first pass through the passage and/or reads 49 or fewer words correct per minute. Provide Extra Practice lessons and retest, and/or provide a Jell-Well Review.

In Unit 26 a Strong Pass/Pass/Weak Pass/No Pass system is implemented. By this level, students who score a Strong Pass are gaining fluency rapidly with little effort. For these students, shorten the per-unit instructional time or skip units that introduce consonants.

- Consistent Strong Passes signal the possibility of moving faster and skipping some consonant units.

- A Pass signals an appropriate pace of instruction.

- A Weak Pass indicates the need for additional work to achieve mastery.

  Weak Passes on two consecutive units are an indication that future difficulties are likely without intervention. With repeated Weak Passes, the student's burden of learning will eventually become overwhelming.

- A No Pass indicates the need for immediate intervention.

Intervention

Continue to provide intervention as needed. In Units 16–38, students who are accurate sometimes fail to gain fluency without added assistance.

Research Snapshot

ORAL READING FLUENCY

Research has shown that oral reading fluency can be a stronger measure of comprehension than traditionally used classroom assessments for reading comprehension. Fuchs, Fuchs, and Maxwell (1988) found a significantly higher correlation between oral reading fluency and the Comprehension Subtest of the Stanford Reading Achievement Test than for traditional direct measures of comprehension (e.g., question answering, passage recall, and cloze).

Samuels and Flor (1997) explain the power of oral reading fluency in reading comprehension. "It is the development of automatic processing in reading that allows our mind to naturally make connections to other prior experiences or knowledge while reading, that allows questions and hypotheses to emerge, and that gives us the ability to pause as we read and to reflect on deeper meanings . . . " (p. 119).

This flow chart demonstrates how to plan instruction based on student performance.

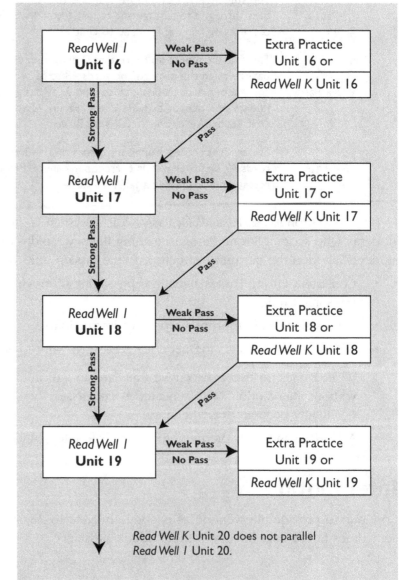

JELL-WELL REVIEW

If students score a No Pass on two consecutive units, consider a quick review of previous units. See Section 5.

Diagnostic-Prescriptive Teaching

SPECIFIC PRESCRIPTIONS FOR UNITS 16–38	
If students have difficulty with . . .	**Then try these prescriptions . . .**
Reading Accurately	Focus on reducing careless errors, repetitions, and self-corrections during oral reading. Follow these steps: a. Provide an Extra Practice lesson. b. After students read the story, have the children listen to you read. Tell students that they can raise their hands (or mark their stories with a simple slash) when they hear you make an error. Model each of the following types of errors: • Reading a word incorrectly • Leaving out a word Explain that it is important to read words accurately and only once. Tell students they should also count the following as errors: • Making corrections • Repeating a word Read the passage slowly. Make errors and ham it up. The children will love it. c. Have students read the passage with individual turns on sentences. Quietly count errors. d. After the reading is complete, review the errors without identifying individuals. Have students practice reading the sentences accurately. Have students reread the passage. The goal is to improve students' accuracy. e. Acknowledge accomplishments.

SPECIFIC PRESCRIPTIONS FOR UNITS 16–38 *(continued)*	
If students have difficulty with . . .	**Then try these prescriptions . . .**
Tricky Words Spelling and Discrimination Practice 	Follow these steps for correcting problems with "where" and "were." • Days 1–2: Write "wHere" on the board. Have the class orally spell "where" by letter names, saying the <u>H</u> loudly. Practice each time the class lines up. • Day 3: Have five students write a "where" question on the board for the class to read and answer. • Day 4: Have each student write "where" on the board or during white board practice. • Day 5: Make a color shade. Find a simple blackline drawing. Draw lines in the picture, creating shapes that can be colored. Write "where" in all the spaces. Draw shapes in the space outside the picture. Write "were" in each of these shapes. Make a copy for each child. Have students color all the spaces with "where." • Days 6–7: Practice spelling "where" *and* "were" orally. Repeat Days 3–5 using "where" and "were."

Fluency
 	
Extending Units With Repeated Readings
	a. Extend lessons (e.g., if students are working on 6-Day Plans, implement 8-Day Plans). Spend more time on repeated readings of Solo Stories.
	  • After practicing the Solo Story with choral reading and individual turns on sentences, give each student a turn to read a page.
	  • Set an accuracy goal of 0–2 errors.
	  • To motivate practice, give each student a transparency and a marker. Have students follow along and mark errors as individuals take turns. Have the strongest readers read first. Model giving compliments. Have one or two students give a compliment to each child.
	
	b. Set up repeated reading sessions with a tutor.
	  • Set an accuracy goal of 0–2 errors.
	  • Have the student read an *easy* Solo Story for accuracy.
	  • When the student is able to read within the accuracy goal, time the passage reading.
	  • Congratulate the child each time his or her fluency improves.
	
	Beginning with Unit 11, Extra Practice Activity 2 includes a chart and story for repeated reading practice. Also see *Getting Started: A Guide to Implementation* for additional charting options.

Washington School Example—
First Grade, Group 2

GROUP ASSESSMENT RECORD   **UNITS 16–25**

Directions

Group Name _____ Group 2 _____

1. Write the Wcpm for a Strong Pass (SP) in the space provided at the top of the fifth column. (This number is found in the bottom box of the Student Assessment Record and provides an overall goal for instruction.)
2. In the third column, record the number of Tricky Words missed. (List the words at the bottom of the form for reteaching.)
3. For the Passage Accuracy Score (fourth column), record the number of errors the student made the first time he or she read through the whole passage (excluding the title). Do not count any additional errors made if the student begins reading the passage a second time.
4. For the Oral Reading Fluency Score, record the number of words read correctly in one minute minus the number of all errors made during that minute.
5. Using the guide on each Student Assessment Record, determine and record a Strong Pass, Weak Pass, or No Pass.
6. For students who do not pass, provide additional practice and retest. Record retest scores to the right of the original scores.

Student Names	Unit 19 / Date	Tricky Word Errors	Passage Accuracy Score Goal 0–2 Errors	Oral Reading Fluency Score SP Goal 44 WCPM	Unit 20 / Date	Tricky Word Errors	Passage Accuracy Score Goal 0–2 Errors	Oral Reading Fluency Score SP Goal 46 WCPM
Tamela	(SP)/ WP / NP	0	0	65	SP / WP / NP	0	0	66
Dominic	(SP)/ WP / NP	0	0	78	SP / WP / NP	0	1	75
Paulino	(SP)/ WP / NP	0	1	45	SP / WP / NP	0	2	46
Amira	(SP)/ WP / NP	0	0	69	SP / WP / NP	0	0	69
Sylvia	(SP)/ WP / NP	0	1	72	SP / WP / NP	0	1	73
Steven	(SP)/ WP / NP	0	0	70	SP / WP / NP	0	0	73
Bethany	(SP)/ WP / NP	0	1	44	SP / WP / NP	0	0	46
	SP / WP / NP				SP / WP / NP			
	SP / WP / NP							

The WCPM Goal should be 44 words or more for this unit. Higher numbers are better.

Prescriptions for Group 2

Tamela, Dominic, Paulino, Amira, Sylvia, Steven, Bethany

Background: The seven students in this group completed *Read Well K*, Unit 17 in kindergarten. In the fall, placement results indicated the children had maintained skills over the summer. The group began first grade instruction in the fall with *Read Well 1*, Unit 16. The group is easily completing units in four or five days.

Projection: Teachers anticipate that the group will complete Unit 38 in late January, thus completing the *Read Well 1* core program. The children will continue into *Read Well Plus*, which means they will be reading significantly above grade level by the end of the year.

First Grade: As shown in the assessment results, all students are maintaining Strong Passes. However, Paulino and Bethany have fluency scores that are significantly lower than others in the group. Mr. Scott has noted that Paulino and Bethany often respond after the group has responded. Mr. Scott recognizes that without assistance, the children will lose confidence and eventually have difficulty staying with this group.

> **INCREASING PRACTICE**
> **Decreasing Group Range**
>
> If a child is struggling compared with others in the group, intervene quickly. Increased practice often makes it possible to maintain group membership in a faster-moving group.

Paulino and Bethany

Background: Paulino is bilingual—speaking both English and Spanish with good proficiency. Spanish is spoken in the home. Bethany is a strong student but has little support from home.

Intervention: Mr. Scott considers regrouping Bethany and Paulino, but the next group down is too low. Tutors and paraprofessionals have no additional time to preteach lessons.

Mr. Scott arranges for Bethany and Paulino to Partner Read each day while their class is lining up and walking to music, P.E., and library. A study station is set up in the classroom (e.g., a desk and two chairs in a quiet corner). As soon as the class *begins* getting ready for music, P.E., or library, Bethany and Paulino will be excused to Partner Read.

The pair is given a box with a timer, a die, a notebook for each child, and two highlighters. The notebooks include Homework Stories and Decoding Reviews for Units 12–20.

Mr. Scott has the children fill out personal goal setting forms. Each child's goal is to improve his or her oral reading fluency score by five words per minute. During a couple of recesses, Mr. Scott teaches the children how to follow these directions:

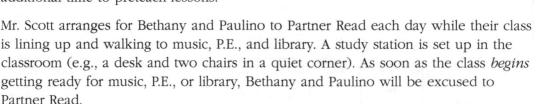

1. Open your notebooks. Practice highlighted words.
2. Roll the die to see who gets to read first.
3. Set the timer for five minutes.
4. Reader 1 reads the first page.
   Reader 2 follows along and marks errors with a highlighter.
   Reader 2 reads the next page.
   Reader 1 follows along and marks errors with a highlighter.
   Take turns reading until the timer rings.
5. Mark where you are with a sticky note. Try to read further the next day.
6. Walk together to P.E., music, or library.
7. Meet Mr. Scott. Then slip quietly into your class.

Mr. Scott tells the children he is very proud of them. They are responsible enough to practice independently, take care of their materials, and meet him on their way to P.E., music, or library.

Periodically, Mr. Scott meets with the children briefly during recess to do one-minute timings on stories they've practiced. Mr. Scott charts the children's oral reading fluency on a graph so they can see their improvement. If one child makes an improvement, both children are given a card. When they have 20 cards, the children are each given a *Read Well* book to keep. (Washington School's PTA has purchased extra *Read Well* storybooks for children to earn.)

Using a Decoding Diagnosis

At Unit 16, the Oral Reading Fluency measure takes the place of the Decoding Assessment. If a student has difficulty meeting the Oral Reading Fluency goal, additional diagnostic information may be of use in determining how to remediate skill deficiencies. A Decoding Diagnosis is included after each of the critical assessments in Units 19–38.

Note: If a student is unable to meet the Oral Reading Fluency goal, he or she may have been misplaced initially, or instruction may have proceeded too fast in the earlier units. If the student makes errors related to one or two skills, you may be able to remediate these skills with intensive work. However, if the student is weak on three or more skills, he or she will need either a careful Jell-Well Review or placement in a lower group.

Guidelines for Remediating Specific Skills

Sounds

- If the student misses only one sound, continue to the next unit but provide additional practice on that sound.
- If the student makes more than one error, consider placing the student in a lower group, providing a Jell-Well Review, or systematically reintroducing one new difficult sound at a time.

Vowel Discrimination

- Have the student practice words that require vowel discrimination. Build lists of words composed of known sounds, in which only the vowel changes (e.g., m<u>e</u>t, m<u>a</u>t, m<u>ea</u>t). See the subtest examples.
- Provide additional practice on all the vowel sounds taught to date. Reteach all vowel units, while continuously reviewing all known sounds.

Beginning Quick Sounds

- Have the student practice pairs of rhyming words in which one word begins with a quick sound (e.g., went-<u>d</u>ent, sand-<u>h</u>and).
- Have the student practice lists of words that begin with one quick sound (e.g., had-hid-hard).
- Reteach all units that introduce a quick sound and review all known sounds.

Blends and Word Endings

- Have the student read lists of words that increase in length and that include difficult blends and/or word endings (e.g., ack-nack-snack, kitt-kitten).
- Dictate words that build up (e.g., in, ink, rink, drink).

Tricky Words

- Identify the difficult words and increase practice on one difficult word at a time.
- Have the student write any difficult word and use it in a sentence.

Washington School Example— First Grade, Transfer Student

Chad transferred into Washington School in the early winter. He knew all of the letter names, all consonant sounds, the short vowel a, many sight words, and he was able to read predictable books that he had rehearsed. After enrollment at Washington School, Chad placed in Unit 10.

At the time of Chad's transfer, Groups 6 and 7 had been merged and were working in Unit 16. Group 8 was in Unit 9, working at a very slow pace. Teachers were reticent to place Chad with Group 8 because he did not have the special needs of children in this group. He was placed in the merged Group 6–7. Chad received a No Pass in Units 16, 17, 18, and 19. While working in Units 17, 18, and 19, Chad received a second dose of reading instruction with a paraprofessional who pretaught the upcoming lesson. At Unit 19, the school reading coach gave Chad the Unit 19 Decoding Diagnosis. Results are shown below.

UNIT 19 DECODING DIAGNOSIS   **ADMINISTRATION**

SOUNDS

ĕ	Th	r	k	oo	E	ar	wh
ĭ̶ (ĕ)	sh	ee	Wh	a	ĕ	H	ĕ̶a (ĕ)

VOWEL DISCRIMINATION

set	sat	s~~i~~t (set)	s~~ea~~t (sent)
Mark	Mick	Mack	m~~ee~~k (make)

BEGINNING QUICK SOUNDS

dent	hand	test	dark
b~~i~~t (hat)	tent	Kim	d~~a~~sh (dish)

BLENDS AND WORD ENDINGS

T~~r~~ish Tr-(Assist)	snack	cr~~ee~~k c-(Assist)	kitten
scoot	wham	drink	s~~c~~at (sac)

TRICKY WORDS

where	into	as	wouldn't
what	to	There	are

• Have students read from a clean copy of the Decoding Diagnosis. Record incorrect responses on another copy.
• Use information from both the Unit 19 Decoding Assessment and the Unit 19 Decoding Diagnosis to identify specific skill deficits.

     Blackline Master 141

Chad's Decoding Diagnosis Results

Sounds

Chad has benefited from instruction with Group 6–7. He demonstrated knowledge of /oo/ taught at Unit 17, /wh/ taught at Unit 18, and /ĕ/ taught at Unit 19. Chad had difficulty with /i/ and /ea/.

Vowel Discrimination

Chad missed "sit," "seat," and "meek." Errors indicated Chad's difficulty with /i/ and /ea/. In saying "make" for "meek," he also read unfamiliar words based on a previously known sight word—rather than by sounds.

Beginning Quick Sounds

Again, Chad missed the word with the /i/, substituting the familiar sight word "hat" for "hit." For the unfamiliar word "dash," Chad substituted "dish," attempting to use prior knowledge of words rather than sounds to determine the word.

Sound and Word Endings

Chad had difficulty with this subtest, demonstrating his inability to sound out familiar words.

Tricky Words

Chad did well with Tricky Words.

Prescription

The school reading coach decided to keep Chad in Group 6–7 but adjusted the instruction of the paraprofessional. Instead of preteaching, the paraprofessional went back to Unit 10. She spent three days on Unit 10 where /i/ was introduced, three days on Unit 13 where /ea/ was introduced, and one day on units that introduced a consonant. In each unit, she worked heavily on the vowels and blending. She skipped Duet Stories and rehearsed Solo Stories with the goal of accuracy. Chad also began Partner Reading Solo Stories with a student in Group 5—good practice for both Chad and his partner.

Within a month, Chad began passing assessments with his group—though still at the lower end of the desired fluency. He should continue with Partner Reading and working on Homework Stories outside of school.

SECTION 5

Jell-Well Reviews

This section explains how to set up a Jell-Well Review, which takes students back to previous units for a fun review and firming-up of knowledge.

Blackline masters are included for Jell-Well Review Planners 1 and 2.

Children With Special Needs

INSTRUCTIONAL SKILLS

When students struggle, it is important that teachers and support staff receive in-depth training to function as specialists for students at risk of reading difficulties.

Work with your colleagues to determine whether additional training and collaboration would be of benefit. Then seek administrative support. Go to www.ReadWell.net for updates on training and professional development opportunities.

Overview and Planning

What Is a Jell-Well Review?

A Jell-Well Review is the *Read Well* term for a review of earlier units. A Jell-Well Review is a period of time taken to celebrate what children have learned and an opportunity to firm up their foundation of learning.

Why Is a Jell-Well Review Needed?

When children enter school with little or no literacy background, or are among the few children for whom learning to read is extremely difficult, a periodic review of earlier units is sometimes necessary. Without a periodic Jell-Well Review, some children simply become overwhelmed with the process of learning new skills.

When to Do a Jell-Well Review

When a student (or group of students) scores two consecutive Weak Passes or a single No Pass, consider regrouping or implementing a Jell-Well Review. Your discretion is needed. For example, if a student receives a No Pass because of repeated errors on a single word, this student would *not* be a candidate for a Jell-Well Review. This student should proceed with a simple correction of the word. On the other hand, if a student scores two consecutive Weak Passes resulting from a lack of fluency, a quick review of previous units can prevent later difficulties.

HOW TO SCHEDULE A JELL-WELL REVIEW

Who . . .	The Best Option . . .	When Resources Are Not Available For A Double Dose . . .
Entire small group	During scheduled instruction and during a second dose of instruction	During scheduled instruction
Part of a group	During a second dose of instruction	Regroup or . . . Provide part of the group with a short Jell-Well Review during the first 10 minutes of scheduled group lessons.
An individual	During a second dose of instruction	Regroup

How to Plan a Jell-Well Review

Follow the steps below in combination with the directions on Planner 1 for Units 1–15 or Planner 2 for Units 16–38. (See pages 117–118.)

1. **Record assessment results at the top of the Jell-Well Planner.**

   List students with strong assessment results first. Then list students who would benefit from a Jell-Well Review.

2. **Determine where to start the Jell-Well Review.**
   - Find the last unit in which all children received a 100% (Units 1–5), or the last unit in which all children received a Strong Pass (Units 6–38) and start the Jell-Well Review with the next unit.
   - For groups that are mixed in skill deficits, go back to the last easy vowel unit. Start the Jell-Well Review there. Skip easy units (usually consonant units). Review all difficult units (usually vowel units). Slow the rate of the review when the skills become more difficult, either by extending the number of days spent on each unit and/or by reviewing all consecutive units.

Jell-Well Planner I

For use with Units 1–15

Planning Information Instructor _____Miles_____   Group _____Anacondas_____   Grade(s) ___1___

Last Unit Completed __10__   Last Unit All Students Completed With 100% or a Strong Pass ___3___

Assessment Results/Comments

Strong Passes 1-10: Summer, Raven, Henry, Yetty: Try moving up to next group; double dose in interim

Natalie   Strong Passes 1-7, <u>Weak Pass 8</u>, Strong Pass 9 with reteaching, No Pass 10: Has never mastered Smooth Blending

Arnie   Strong Passes 1-3, <u>Weak Pass 4</u>, Weak Pass 5, Weak Pass 6 with reteaching, Weak Pass 7, Weak Pass 8 with preteaching, Weak Pass 9 with preteaching, No Pass 10: Struggles with vowel /a/ and /i/, says name instead of sound

Matilde   Strong Passes 1-8, <u>Weak Pass 9</u>, Weak Pass 10: Difficulty with words ending in s and blending /ti/

George   Strong Passes 1-8, <u>Weak Pass 9</u>, No Pass 10: Absent many days; says /tuh/ and /wuh/—difficulty causing blending problems, calls short /iii/ by the letter name

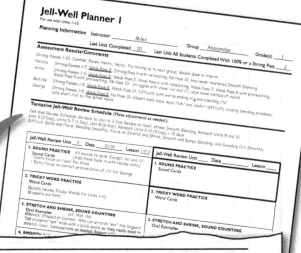
3. Plan diagnostically.

Analyze the items each student missed or self-corrected on assessments; list error patterns with each student's name. The pinpointed skills provide a guide for instructional emphasis. For the purpose of maintenance and increased fluency, practice should cover all skills in a review unit.

Some students will be accurate, but not fluent. Fluency is important as it reflects depth of knowledge. For students who are accurate but dysfluent, practice on easy skills is required to build speed of recognition and increased access to comprehension.

4. Set up a tentative schedule for review with the number of days planned per unit.

- Plan a 1-Day Review for units that introduced easy skills for students (generally, easy consonant sounds).

- Plan 2- or 3-Day Reviews for units that introduce difficult skills for students (generally, vowels).

- If more time for review is needed, consider reteaching each unit.

(continued)

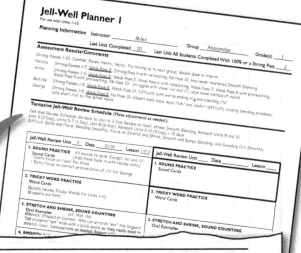

Tentative Jell-Well Review Schedule (Make adjustments as needed.)

Jell Well Review Schedule: Go back to Unit 4, 2-Day Review on /aaa/, stress Smooth Blending, Reteach Units 9 and 10.
Unit 4 (2-Day), Units 5–7 (1-Day), Unit 8 (2-Day), Reteach Units 9–10 (4-Day) = 15 days
Difficult Skills and Focus: Blending Smoothly, focus on Stretch and Shrink, Smooth and Bumpy Blending, and Sounding Out Smoothly

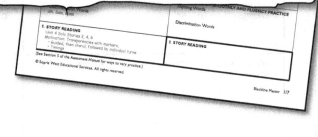

5. Develop lesson plans for each day of the Jell-Well Review.

You can use:

• The review unit's Extra Practice lessons, or

• The appropriate Jell-Well Review Planner.

Use the review unit's Decoding Practice 1–4 (Decoding Practice 4, in particular) as a source for words and word lists.

Use the review unit's Solo Stories, Homework, and Extra Practice for repeated reading practice.

Jell-Well Review Unit __4__ Date __10/18__ Lesson _1 of 2_	Jell-Well Review Unit ____ Date _____ Lesson ____
I. SOUND PRACTICE All sounds to date: Except /w/ and /i/. Sound Cards (Add these back in with review units.) • Extra focus on /aaa/ for Arnie • Extra focus on correct pronunciation of /t/ for George	**I. SOUND PRACTICE** Sound Cards
2. TRICKY WORD PRACTICE Word Cards Quickly review Tricky Words for Units 1–10. Students are firm.	**2. TRICKY WORD PRACTICE** Word Cards
3. STRETCH AND SHRINK, SOUND COUNTING Oral Examples sat, that, did Gimmick: Stopwatch Contest, Who can stretch "sat" the longest? Tell students "sat" ends with a quick sound so they really need to stretch /aaa/. Demonstrate as needed. Repeat with each word.	**3. STRETCH AND SHRINK, SOUND COUNTING** Oral Examples
4. SMOOTH AND BUMPY BLENDING Blending Cards Cards 9, 10, 11	**4. SMOOTH AND BUMPY BLENDING** Blending Cards
5. WORD DICTATION Dictation Examples Am, me, Sam, seem	**5. WORD DICTATION** Dictation Examples
6. SOUNDING OUT SMOOTHLY AND FLUENCY PRACTICE Rhyming Words ee, me, see Discrimination Words am, Sam, seem	**6. SOUNDING OUT SMOOTHLY AND FLUENCY PRACTICE** Rhyming Words Discrimination Words
7. STORY READING Unit 4 Solo Stories 2, 4, 6 Motivation: Transparencies with markers, • Guided, then choral, followed by individual turns • Timings	**7. STORY READING**

(See Section 5 of the *Assessment Manual* for ways to vary practice.)

Blackline Master 117

Motivating Students

Your biggest challenge is to keep children excited and motivated. When children feel success is unattainable, they often give up. The following guidelines are important during *all* instruction but are critical when working with high-risk readers.

- **To help children understand that success is possible, set informal and quickly attainable goals.**

  For example, if the children are near mastery on a list of words, set an attainable goal. Say something like:

  > Let's see if you can carefully and correctly read all five words in a row.

- **To keep their attention, provide positive contingent descriptive feedback.**

  Contingent descriptive feedback helps children learn exactly *how* they are meeting your expectations and helps them understand how their actions can help them reach their goals. It clarifies for students what they've done correctly and may point out what they've done incorrectly. (With noncontingent praise, a teacher my say "Good job" even though the students missed a word.) The following script illustrates how to provide contingent descriptive feedback.

  In this example, the students are reading the word list; sat, wind, in, sit, and hand. If a student (or students) reads "win" instead of "wind," say something like:

Clarify what the students did right.	You carefully read four words.
Point out what was counterproductive.	But I heard a guess on one word. You forgot to read all the way to the end of the word.
Guide students through a correction.	What was the last sound? (/d/) Sound out the hard word. (/wwwiiinnnd/) Tell me the word. (/wind/)
Restate the attainable goal.	You figured out the word was "wind," not "win." The *wind* blew my hat off. Now let's see if you can read all five words carefully and correctly. (sat, wind, in, sit, hand)
Congratulate students on their accomplishments.	You read all five words correctly.

Motivating Students (*continued*)

- **To help children value their successes, celebrate often.**

  When learning to read is a challenge, children often do not recognize or value their own achievements. Help students learn to recognize and take pride in their accomplishments.

  > You read all five words carefully and correctly! Say, "We did it!" **(We did it.)**

  > Now stand up and take a bow. I'm going to clap for you!

- **To make practice fun, use gimmicks, gadgets, and games while keeping response rates high.** (See the menu on pages 113–116.)

  Young children love routines but they can also get mired in uninspired practice. Add a few creative twists to maintain motivation. Luckily, young children respond to teacher enthusiasm. A stopwatch can be used to turn practice into a game. With the right comments, a colored marker can take on special meaning. "Wow! You can read 'would,' 'could,' and 'should.' I'm going to write 'would,' 'could,' and 'should' for you with my purple marker. You can take the words home and put them on your refrigerator."

Menu of Prescriptions

This list of prescriptions is intended to stimulate your imagination with some fun ways to practice that keep the focus on high response rates. A Jell-Well Review will not be productive unless practice focuses on accuracy and then fluency. See *Getting Started: A Guide to Implementation* for additional suggestions.

> **IMPORTANT**
> Keep practice light and fun, but focused. Restructure any gimmick or game that results in fewer responses.

SOUND PRACTICE		
Gimmick Or Game	**Instructional Focus**	**Procedure**
Timed Reading	Increased fluency with sounds	Use Decoding Practice 4, Sound Review. • Set a goal of one sound per second. Establish a pace and have students practice a Timed Reading of the sounds. Let's see if you can read 30 sounds in 30 seconds. • Once the goal is reached, increase it. Yesterday, you read 30 sounds in 30 seconds. Do you think we can read *35* sounds in 30 seconds today?
Transparencies	Increased attention to difficult sounds by varying the response	Use Decoding Practice 4, Sound Review. • Have each student place a transparency over Decoding Practice 4. • Have students underline any difficult sounds or all vowel sounds. Everyone, underline /sh/. Now underline /i/ . . . • Have students practice the underlined sounds in a different rhythm (two times, three times) or type of voice (loud, soft). Whenever you see an underlined sound, read it two times. Listen to me do the square row: /sh/, /i/-/i/, /r/, /ee/-/ee/, /w/, /c/. Now it's your turn.
Who Can Hold the Sound the Longest?	Increased accuracy	Use Sound Cards. • Put a paper clip on the difficult sound as a signal. • When the paper-clipped card comes up in Sound Card Practice, practice the sound, then see who can hold the sound the longest without taking a breath. There's the hard sound. My turn. Listen. /iii/. Your turn. (/iiiiii/) Now let's see who can hold /iii/ the longest. Remember, when you take a breath, you're out.

(continued)

SOUND PRACTICE (*continued*)		
Sticky Notes	Distributed Practice—practice throughout the day	At the end of the lesson, give each child a special sticky note with his or her special sound or Tricky Word written on it. Roberto, you worked hard and learned /iii/ today. I'm going to write your special sound on this sticky note. What sound? (/iii/) Yes, /iii/ as in insect. Put it on your desk. When I go by your desk, you can tell me what it says. If you don't play with it, you can take the note home and keep it.

Prevent guessing. Identify words missed and error patterns. Every time the student reads a Tricky Word incorrectly, he or she is reinforcing an error pattern.

TRICKY WORD PRACTICE		
Gimmick or Game	**Instructional Focus**	**Procedure**
Don't Let the Tricky Word Fool You!	Increased accuracy	Use Tricky Word Cards. • Identify a difficult word. Write the word (e.g., want) on additional cards. • Put a paper clip on each difficult Tricky Word Card as a signal. • Before starting the Tricky Word practice, have students try sounding out the word. Then use the word in a sentence. Our goal is to not let the Tricky Word "want" fool us. Watch for the paper clips. Each paper clip tells us that we need to stop and think, so we don't read the wrong word. Sound out the Tricky Word. (/wwwăăănnnt/) You don't say "I *wănt* a new pencil." What do you say? (I *want* a new pencil.) Tell me the word. (want) • Take the paper clips off the cards and reset the goal. I'm going to take the paper clips off the Tricky Word "want." Don't let it fool you. If you aren't sure of a word, stop and sound it out.
Goodbye Tricky Words (chalkboard game)	Increased accuracy and fluency	Put a column of Tricky Words on the board. There should be more than two difficult words. When students master the list, erase each word. First word. (a) Say goodbye "a." **Erase "a."** Next word. (isn't) Say goodbye "isn't." **Erase "isn't."** Next word. (wasn't) Say goodbye "wasn't." **Erase "wasn't."** Next word. (want) Say goodbye "want." **Erase "want."**

STRETCH AND SHRINK		
Gimmick or Game	**Instructional Focus**	**Procedure**
Stopwatch Contest, Timed Stretches	Phonemic Awareness—training to facilitate Sounding Out Smoothly	• Have fun helping students really *ssstrrrrrreeeeeetch* the words out smoothly. • After practicing, tell students they can play a game to see who can stretch a word the longest. Let's see who can stretch "sad" the longest. It ends with a quick sound so you really need to stretch /sss/ and /aaa/ a long time. Let's time me first. Listen. /sssssssaaaaad/ That was five seconds. Who can do it even longer? Remember, don't stop between the sounds.

SMOOTH AND BUMPY BLENDING		
Gimmick or Game	**Instructional Focus**	**Procedure**
Catch the Teacher	Phonemic Awareness—training to facilitate Sounding Out Smoothly	• Copy a list of pattern words from a Decoding Practice onto the chalkboard. • Tell students they get to try to catch you doing Bumpy Blending. Listen to me sound out a word. If I do Smooth Blending, give me a thumbs up. If you catch me doing Bumpy Blending, say "Bump, bump, bump!"

ACCURACY AND FLUENCY		
Gimmick or Game	**Instructional Focus**	**Procedure**
Transparencies	Increased accuracy	• Have each student place a transparency over Decoding Practice 4. • Have students underline each letter that changes on a list. • Have students read each underlined letter three times and then read the whole word. • Have students practice the list for fluency. • When the list is mastered by the group and individuals, have students cross out the list, draw happy faces, or draw stars.

(continued)

ACCURACY AND FLUENCY *(continued)*		
Word Charts and Pointers	Increased accuracy and fluency	• Copy lists from the review unit's Decoding Practice onto large flip charts and color code any difficult words. • Have students lead the practice using a pointer with a fun toy on the end (e.g, a plastic fly for Unit 20 with /-y/ as in "fly"). [Marshall], you were sitting up and paying attention. You get to be the teacher. Here's the pointer. Which column would you like to teach? **As the student points, provide verbal prompts for each response.** Everyone, watch [Marshall's] pointer. First word. (man)

Work diagnostically with repeated readings. See *Getting Started: A Guide to Implementation* for a longer list of ways to increase fluency through repeated readings.

STORY READING		
Gimmick or Game	**Instructional Focus**	**Procedure**
Starred Words One-to-One	Units 1–6 Heavily guided practice (Fluency isn't relevant in the early units, but some students have difficulty getting the sounding out process going as they try to read short sentences.)	Use Homework or Extra Practice passages. • Work one-to-one for a few minutes each day. • Work on one sentence at a time. Start sounding out a word just ahead of the student's normal response rate. Fade your voice as the student sounds out the rest of the word, but lead back in to get the student started on the next word. • Have the student immediately repeat the sentence. Draw a star above each word sounded out without your assistance.
Starred Words, Sentences, or Paragraphs	Accuracy, Units 1–38	Use Homework Stories or Extra Practice passages. • Guide a choral reading of the story. • Provide individual turns while others whisper read and follow each word with their fingers. While an individual reads, draw stars on the student's story directly above *each* word read correctly without guessing or self-correcting. Accept and encourage sounding out. • Provide additional attempts as time allows. (For students in higher units, draw stars at the end of sentences or paragraphs.)

Jell-Well Planner 1

For use with Units 1–15

Planning Information Instructor _____ Group _____ Grade(s) _____

Last Unit Completed _____ Last Unit All Students Completed With 100% or a Strong Pass _____

Assessment Results/Comments

Tentative Jell-Well Review Schedule (Make adjustments as needed.)

Jell-Well Review Unit ____ Date _____ Lesson ____	Jell-Well Review Unit ____ Date _____ Lesson ____
I. SOUND PRACTICE Sound Cards	**I. SOUND PRACTICE** Sound Cards
2. TRICKY WORD PRACTICE Word Cards	**2. TRICKY WORD PRACTICE** Word Cards
3. STRETCH AND SHRINK, SOUND COUNTING Oral Examples	**3. STRETCH AND SHRINK, SOUND COUNTING** Oral Examples
4. SMOOTH AND BUMPY BLENDING Blending Cards	**4. SMOOTH AND BUMPY BLENDING** Blending Cards
5. WORD DICTATION Dictation Examples	**5. WORD DICTATION** Dictation Examples
6. SOUNDING OUT SMOOTHLY AND FLUENCY PRACTICE Rhyming Words Discrimination Words	**6. SOUNDING OUT SMOOTHLY AND FLUENCY PRACTICE** Rhyming Words Discrimination Words
7. STORY READING	**7. STORY READING**

(See Section 5 of the *Assessment Manual* for ways to vary practice.)

Jell-Well Planner 2

For use with Units 16–38

Planning Information   Instructor _____   Group _____   Grade(s) _____

Last Unit Completed _____   Fluency Goal in Last Unit Completed _____WCPM

Last Unit All Students Completed With 100% or a Strong Pass _____

Assessment Results/Comments

Tentative Jell-Well Review Schedule (Make adjustments as needed.)

Jell-Well Review Unit ____ Date _____ Lesson ____	Jell-Well Review Unit ____ Date _____ Lesson ____
I. SOUND PRACTICE Sound Cards or Sound Practice, Decoding Practice 4	**I. SOUND PRACTICE** Sound Cards or Sound Practice, Decoding Practice 4
2. TRICKY WORD PRACTICE Word Cards	**2. TRICKY WORD PRACTICE** Word Cards
3. STRETCH AND SHRINK, SMOOTH AND BUMPY BLENDING Short Vowel Words	**3. STRETCH AND SHRINK, SMOOTH AND BUMPY BLENDING** Short Vowel Words
4. WORD DICTATION Dictation Examples	**4. WORD DICTATION** Dictation Examples
5. ACCURACY AND FLUENCY PRACTICE Rhyming Words Discrimination Words Multisyllabic Words	**5. ACCURACY AND FLUENCY PRACTICE** Rhyming Words Discrimination Words Multisyllabic Words
6. STORY READING	**6. STORY READING**

(See Section 5 of the *Assessment Manual* for ways to vary practice.)

SECTION 6

Assessments and Forms

This section includes the end-of-unit administration and recordkeeping forms.

Permission to reprint the assessments and record forms is provided on the copyright page of this manual.

SUBTEST A. TRACKING AND WORDS

GOAL 5/5

SUBTEST B. SMOOTH AND BUMPY BLENDING

GOAL 2/2

SUBTEST C. FINGER TRACKING

GOAL 4/4

SUBTEST D. COMPREHENSION

Read the story to the student. Ask: Who is the story about?

GOAL 1/1

This is Olivia. Olivia lives in the city.

Olivia lives in an apartment.

SCORING	If the student needs assistance, the item is incorrect.
PASS	The student meets the goals on all subtests. Proceed to Unit B.
NO PASS	The student fails to meet the goal on one or more subtests. Seek consultation. Consider providing instruction in *Read Well K*, Preludes A–F.

SUBTEST A. TRACKING, SOUNDS, AND WORDS   GOAL 5/5

SUBTEST B. SMOOTH AND BUMPY BLENDING   GOAL 4/4

SUBTEST C. FINGER TRACKING   GOAL 4/4

SUBTEST D. COMPREHENSION

Read the story to the student. Ask: Who is the story about?   GOAL 1/1

This is Roberto.

Roberto's class is learning about snakes.

SCORING   If the student needs assistance, the item is incorrect.

PASS   The student meets the goals on all subtests. Proceed to Unit 1.

NO PASS   The student fails to meet the goal on one or more subtests.
Seek consultation. Consider providing instruction in *Read Well K*, Preludes A–F.

SUBTEST A. SOUNDS AND WORDS   GOAL 4/4

S   I   I   S

SUBTEST B. SMOOTH AND BUMPY BLENDING   GOAL 4/4

S S S   SSS   I I I   III

SUBTEST C. FINGER TRACKING   GOAL 4/4

I   s   S   I

SUBTEST D. COMPREHENSION   GOAL 2/2

Read the story to the student. Ask: Who is the story about? What is she doing?

Snake went visiting in her brand new skin, but the sheep ran away. The hen ran away,

and the farmer's wife screamed.

Snake said, "I'm really very nice." Then Snake smiled and winked.

SCORING	If the student needs assistance, the item is incorrect.
PASS	The student meets the goals on all subtests. Proceed to Unit 2.
NO PASS	The student fails to meet the goal on 1 or more subtests. Provide Extra Practice lessons and retest. Consider providing instruction in Units A and B. See the *Assessment Manual* for additional information.

SUBTEST A. SOUNDS   GOAL 4/4

ee   s   e   S

SUBTEST B. SMOOTH AND BUMPY BLENDING   GOAL 4/4

e   e   e   eee   s ee   see

SUBTEST C. TRICKY WORD   GOAL 1/1

I

SUBTEST D. SENTENCE   GOAL 2/2

I see.

SCORING   If the student needs assistance, the item is incorrect.

PASS   The student meets the goals on all subtests. Proceed to Unit 3.

NO PASS   The student fails to meet the goal on 1 or more subtests. Provide additional practice and retest. Consider the student for instruction in Units A and B. See the *Assessment Manual* for additional information.

SUBTEST A. SOUNDS

GOAL 5/6

m   S   e   M   ee   s

SUBTEST B. SMOOTH AND BUMPY BLENDING

GOAL 4/4

m m m   mmm   m e   me

SUBTEST C. TRICKY WORD (AND I'M)

GOAL 2/2

I   I'm

SUBTEST D. SENTENCE

GOAL 3/3

I see me.

SCORING   If the student needs assistance the item is incorrect.
PASS   The student meets the goals on all subtests. Proceed to Unit 4.
NO PASS   The student fails to meet the goal on 1 or more subtests. Provide Extra Practice and retest, and/or provide a Jell-Well Review.
See the *Assessment Manual* for additional information.

SUBTEST A. SOUNDS GOAL 5/6

a M e s m A

SUBTEST B. SOUNDING OUT SMOOTHLY GOAL 3/4

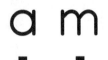 

SUBTEST C. TRICKY WORD (AND I'M) GOAL 2/2

I'm I

SUBTEST D. SENTENCES GOAL 5/5

See me.

I am Sam.

SCORING	If the student needs assistance, the item is incorrect.
PASS	The student meets the goals on all subtests. Proceed to Unit 5.
NO PASS	The student fails to meet the goal on 1 or more subtests. Provide Extra Practice lessons and retest, and/or provide a Jell-Well Review. See the *Assessment Manual* for additional information.

SUBTEST A. SOUNDS   GOAL 5/6

D   a   s   ee   d   M

SUBTEST B. SMOOTH AND BUMPY BLENDING   GOAL 2/2

a   m   am

SUBTEST C. SOUNDING OUT SMOOTHLY   GOAL 4/4

dad   me   add   seed

SUBTEST D. TRICKY WORDS   GOAL 2/2

said   I

SUBTEST E. SENTENCES   GOAL 6/6

I'm mad.

Dad said, "I see."

SCORING   If the student needs assistance the item is incorrect.
PASS   The student meets the goals on all subtests. Proceed to Unit 6.
NO PASS   The student fails to meet the goal on 1 or more subtests. Provide Extra Practice lessons and retest, and/or provide a a Jell-Well Review.

SUBTEST A. SOUNDS   GOAL 5/6

A   th   d   e   m   D

SUBTEST B. SMOOTH AND BUMPY BLENDING   GOAL 2/2

Dad   Dad

SUBTEST C. SOUNDING OUT SMOOTHLY   GOAL 3/4

am   see   Dad   seeds

SUBTEST D. TRICKY WORDS (AND I'M)   GOAL 3/3

the   I'm   said

SUBTEST E. SENTENCES ★Desired Fluency: 20 seconds or less   GOAL 7/8

I said, "See the .

See sad Sam."

SCORING	If the student needs assistance, the item is incorrect.
STRONG PASS	The student meets the goals on all subtests and has attained the desired fluency. Proceed to Unit 7.
WEAK PASS	The student meets the goals on 4 out of 5 subtests and/or fails to attain the desired fluency. Proceed to Unit 7 with added practice, or provide Extra Practice in Unit 6, and/or provide a Jell-Well Review.
NO PASS	The student fails to meet the goals on 2 or more subtests. Provide Extra Practice and retest, and/or provide a Jell-Well Review.

SUBTEST A. SOUNDS   GOAL 5/6

N a d n ee th

SUBTEST B. SMOOTH AND BUMPY BLENDING   GOAL 2/2

a n d   and

SUBTEST C. SOUNDING OUT SMOOTHLY   GOAL 3/4

need   an   seen   than

SUBTEST D. TRICKY WORDS (AND I'M)   GOAL 3/3

said   I'm   the

SUBTEST E. SENTENCES   Desired Fluency: 20 seconds or less (24 wCPM)   GOAL 7/8

I need Dan.

"See Nan," said the man.

SCORING	If the student needs assistance, the item is incorrect.
STRONG PASS	The student meets the goals on all subtests and has attained the desired fluency. Proceed to Unit 8.
WEAK PASS	The student meets the goals on 4 out of 5 subtests and/or fails to attain the desired fluency. Proceed to Unit 8 with added practice, or provide Extra Practice in Unit 7, and/or provide a Jell-Well Review.
NO PASS	The student fails to meet the goals on 2 or more subtests. Provide Extra Practice and retest, and/or provide a Jell-Well Review.

CRITICAL ASSESSMENT

SUBTEST A. SOUNDS   GOAL 5/6

t   N   e   T   a   th

SUBTEST B. SMOOTH AND BUMPY BLENDING   GOAL 2/2

SUBTEST C. SOUNDING OUT SMOOTHLY   GOAL 3/4

at   seed   ants   Dad

SUBTEST D. TRICKY WORDS   GOAL 3/3

I   the   said

SUBTEST E. SENTENCES Desired Fluency: 20 seconds or less (27 wcpm)   GOAL 8/9

I sat and sat.

Nan meets Sam and me.

SCORING	If the student needs assistance, the item is incorrect.
STRONG PASS	The student meets the goals on all subtests and has attained the desired fluency. Proceed to Unit 9.
WEAK PASS	The student meets the goals on 4 out of 5 subtests and/or fails to attain the desired fluency. Proceed to Unit 9 with added practice, or provide Extra Practice in Unit 8, and/or provide a Jell-Well Review.
NO PASS	The student fails to meet the goals on 2 or more subtests. Provide Extra Practice and retest, and/or provide a Jell-Well Review.

SUBTEST A. SOUNDS   **GOAL 5/6**

n   W   M   ee   t   a

SUBTEST B. SOUNDING OUT SMOOTHLY   **GOAL 3/4**

Dan   sand   that   weeds

SUBTEST C. TRICKY WORDS   **GOAL 3/3**

was   said   the

SUBTEST D. SENTENCES   Desired Fluency: 20 seconds or less (30 WCPM)   **GOAL 9/10**

We see weeds.

I see ants and the sad man.

SCORING	If the student needs assistance, the item is incorrect.
STRONG PASS	The student meets the goals on all subtests and has attained the desired fluency. Proceed to Unit 10.
WEAK PASS	The student meets the goals on 3 out of 4 subtests and/or fails to attain the desired fluency. Proceed to Unit 10 with added practice, or provide Extra Practice lessons in Unit 9, and/or provide a Jell-Well Review.
NO PASS	The student fails to meet the goals on 2 or more subtests. Provide Extra Practice lessons and retest, and/or provide a Jell-Well Review.

CRITICAL ASSESSMENT

SUBTEST A. SOUNDS   GOAL 5/6

w   i   N   a   Th   e

SUBTEST B. SOUNDING OUT SMOOTHLY   GOAL 3/4

it   That's   did   seeds

SUBTEST C. TRICKY WORDS (AND I'M)   GOAL 3/3

I'm   was   The

SUBTEST D. SENTENCES   Desired Fluency: 25 seconds or less (29 WCPM)   GOAL 11/12

Tim and I sat in the wind.

We said, "Did Nan win?"

SCORING   If the student needs assistance, the item is incorrect.

STRONG PASS   The student meets the goals on all subtests and has attained the desired fluency. Proceed to Unit 11.

WEAK PASS   The student meets the goals on 3 out of 4 subtests and/or fails to attain the desired fluency. Proceed to Unit 11 with added practice, or provide Extra Practice lessons in Unit 10, and/or provide a Jell-Well Review.

NO PASS   The student fails to meet the goals on 2 or more subtests. Provide Extra Practice lessons and retest, and/or provide a Jell-Well Review.

SUBTEST A. SOUNDS   GOAL 6/7

h	i	W	ee	d	H	a

SUBTEST B. SOUNDING OUT SMOOTHLY   GOAL 4/5

than   had   we   Sam's   swim

SUBTEST C. TRICKY WORDS   GOAL 3/4

as   The   His   was

SUBTEST D. SENTENCES   Desired Fluency: 30 seconds or less (30 WCPM)   GOAL 13/15

He said, "That man is mad."

Nat has seeds.

Sam's hat was in the sand.

SCORING   If the student needs assistance, the item is incorrect.
STRONG PASS   The student meets the goals on all subtests and has attained the desired fluency. Proceed to Unit 12.
WEAK PASS   The student meets the goals on 3 out of 4 subtests and/or fails to attain the desired fluency. Proceed to Unit 12 with added practice, or provide Extra Practice lessons in Unit 11, and/or provide a Jell-Well Review.
NO PASS   The student fails to meet the goals on 2 or more subtests. Provide Extra Practice lessons and retest, and/or provide a Jell-Well Review.

CRITICAL ASSESSMENT

SUBTEST A. SOUNDS   GOAL 6/7

N   H   c   e   h   i   C

SUBTEST B. SOUNDING OUT SMOOTHLY   GOAL 4/5

hid   seen   that   wind   Cass

SUBTEST C. TRICKY WORDS   GOAL 3/4

hasn't   a   his   isn't

SUBTEST D. SENTENCES Desired Fluency: 30 seconds or less (32 WCPM)   GOAL 14/16

Tim swims with his dad.

We can't see a cat.

This can has sand in it.

SCORING	If the student needs assistance, the item is incorrect.
STRONG PASS	The student meets the goals on all subtests and has attained the desired fluency. Proceed to Unit 13.
WEAK PASS	The student meets the goals on 3 out of 4 subtests and/or fails to attain the desired fluency. Proceed to Unit 13 with added practice, or provide Extra Practice lessons in Unit 12, and/or provide a Jell-Well Review.
NO PASS	The student fails to meet the goals on 2 or more subtests. Provide Extra Practice lessons and retest, and/or provide a Jell-Well Review.

SUBTEST A. SOUNDS **GOAL 6/7**

r C a d R ea h

SUBTEST B. SOUNDING OUT SMOOTHLY **GOAL 4/5**

rat He dim can sweet

SUBTEST C. TRICKY WORDS (AND I'M) **GOAL 3/4**

is want I'm has

SUBTEST D. SENTENCES Desired Fluency: 30 seconds or less (34 WCPM) **GOAL 15/17**

The deer ran in the mist.

Nan meets Sam at the tree.

Tad didn't eat with me.

SCORING If the student needs assistance, the item is incorrect.
STRONG PASS The student meets the goals on all subtests and has attained the desired fluency. Proceed to Unit 14.
WEAK PASS The student meets the goals on 3 out of 4 subtests and/or fails to attain the desired fluency. Proceed to Unit 14 with added practice, or provide Extra Practice in Unit 13, and/or provide a Jell-Well Review.
NO PASS The student fails to meet the goals on 2 or more subtests. Provide Extra Practice lessons and retest, and/or provide a Jell-Well Review.

SUBTEST A. SOUNDS   GOAL 6/7

Sh   w   i   r   e   H   c

SUBTEST B. SOUNDING OUT SMOOTHLY   GOAL 4/5

dash   him   tree   Rats   read

SUBTEST C. TRICKY WORDS   GOAL 3/4

should   was   said   want

SUBTEST D. SENTENCES Desired Fluency: 30 seconds or less (36 wcpm)   GOAL 16/18

She would swim in the sea.

We wish we could meet.

The rats should eat a sweet treat.

SCORING   If the student needs assistance, the item is incorrect.
STRONG PASS   The student meets the goals on all subtests and has attained the desired fluency. Proceed to Unit 15.
WEAK PASS   The student meets the goals on 3 out of 4 subtests and/or fails to attain the desired fluency. Proceed to Unit 15 with added practice, or provide Extra Practice in Unit 14, and/or provide a Jell-Well Review.
NO PASS   The student fails to meet the goals on 2 or more subtests. Provide Extra Practice and retest, and/or provide a Jell-Well Review.

CRITICAL ASSESSMENT

SUBTEST A. SOUNDS   GOAL 6/7

| k | a | sh | ea | i | ck | r |

SUBTEST B. SOUNDING OUT SMOOTHLY   GOAL 4/5

creek   She   can't   mean   dish

SUBTEST C. TRICKY WORDS   GOAL 3/4

wants   The   as   said

SUBTEST D. SENTENCES Desired Fluency: 35 seconds or less (36 WCPM)   GOAL 19/21

Kim and Dee would sit in the sand.

Rick couldn't smash that tan hat.

Cass said, "I think this trash stinks."

SCORING	If the student needs assistance, the item is incorrect.
STRONG PASS	The student meets the goals on all subtests and has attained the desired fluency. Proceed to Unit 16.
WEAK PASS	The student meets the goals on 3 out of 4 subtests and/or fails to attain the desired fluency. Proceed to Unit 16 with added practice, or provide Extra Practice in Unit 15, and/or provide a Jell-Well Review.
NO PASS	The student fails to meet the goals on 2 or more subtests. Provide Extra Practice and retest, and/or provide a Jell-Well Review.

TRICKY WORD WARM-UP

| was | to | his | do | shouldn't |

ORAL READING FLUENCY PASSAGE

Did He?

★Did the raccoon think it was meat?   7

Did the moose crash into Mack?   13

Did the deer swim at noon?   19

Did the moon sink too soon?   25

ORAL READING FLUENCY	Start timing at the ★ Mark errors. Make a single slash in the text (/) at 60 seconds. Have student complete passage. If the student completes the passage in less than 60 seconds, have the student go back to the ★ and continue reading. Make a double slash (//) in the text at 60 seconds.
WCPM	Determine words correct per minute by subtracting errors from words read in 60 seconds.
STRONG PASS	The student scores no more than 2 errors on the first pass through the passage and reads a minimum of 36 words correct per minute. Proceed to Unit 17.
WEAK PASS	The student scores no more than 2 errors on the first pass through the passage and reads 28 to 35 words correct per minute. Proceed to Unit 17 with added fluency prsactice, or provide Extra Practice lessons in Unit 16, and/or provide a Jell-Well Review.
NO PASS	The student scores 3 or more errors on the first pass through the passage, and/or reads 27 or fewer words correct per minute. Provide Extra Practice lessons and retest, and/or provide a Jell-Well Review.

TRICKY WORD WARM-UP

are	couldn't	into	a	wants

ORAL READING FLUENCY PASSAGE

Mack's Car

★Mack sat in his car.   5

The car was in a crash.   11

It wouldn't start.   14

Mack had to think hard.   19

Mack said, "I should ask Dad.   25

He's smart."   27

ORAL READING FLUENCY	Start timing at the ★ Mark errors. Make a single slash in the text (/) at 60 seconds. Have student complete passage. If the student completes the passage in less than 60 seconds, have the student go back to the ★ and continue reading. Make a double slash (//) in the text at 60 seconds.
WCPM	Determine words correct per minute by subtracting errors from words read in 60 seconds.
STRONG PASS	The student scores no more than 2 errors on the first pass through the passage and reads a minimum of 39 or more words correct per minute. Proceed to Unit 18.
WEAK PASS	The student scores no more than 2 errors on the first pass through the passage and reads a minimum of 30 to 38 words correct per minute. Proceed to Unit 18 with added fluency practice, or provide Extra Practice lessons in Unit 17, and/or provide a Jell-Well Review.
NO PASS	The student scores 3 or more errors on the first pass through the passage, and/or reads 29 or fewer words correct per minute. Provide Extra Practice lessons and retest, and/or provide a Jell-Well Review.

TRICKY WORD WARM-UP

| What | Into | are | do | has |

ORAL READING FLUENCY PASSAGE

Whoosh! Wham!

★What do I hear?   4

I hear the harsh wind. Whoosh!   10

I hear a tree crash. Wham!   16

What did we do?   20

We hid in the shack.   25

We are smart.   28

ORAL READING FLUENCY	Start timing at the ★ Mark errors. Make a single slash in the text (/) at 60 seconds. Have student complete passage. If the student completes the passage in less than 60 seconds, have the student go back to the ★ and continue reading. Make a double slash (//) in the text at 60 seconds.
WCPM	Determine words correct per minute by subtracting errors from words read in 60 seconds.
STRONG PASS	The student scores no more than 2 errors on the first pass through the passage and reads a minimum of 42 or more words correct per minute. Proceed to Unit 19.
WEAK PASS	The student scores no more than 2 errors on the first pass through the passage and reads a minimum of 32 to 41 words correct per minute. Proceed to 19 with added fluency practice, or provide Extra Practice lessons in Unit 18, and/or provide a Jell-Well Review.
NO PASS	The student scores 3 or more errors on the first pass through the passage, and/or reads 31 or fewer words correct per minute. Provide Extra Practice lessons and retest, and/or provide a Jell-Well Review.

CRITICAL ASSESSMENT

TRICKY WORD WARM-UP

| there | what | his | want | are |

ORAL READING FLUENCY PASSAGE

Where to Rest?

★The red hen went to ask the cat   8

where she should rest.   12

The cat said, "This shed is   18

dark and neat."   21

"Thanks!" said the hen. "That's   26

what I need."   29

ORAL READING FLUENCY	Start timing at the ★. Mark errors. Make a single slash in the text (/) at 60 seconds. Have student complete passage. If the student completes the passage in less than 60 seconds, have the student go back to the ★ and continue reading. Make a double slash (//) in the text at 60 seconds.
WCPM	Determine words correct per minute by subtracting errors from words read in 60 seconds.
STRONG PASS	The student scores no more than 2 errors on the first pass through the passage and reads a minimum of 44 or more words correct per minute. Proceed to Unit 20.
WEAK PASS	The student scores no more than 2 errors on the first pass through the passage and reads a minimum of 34 to 43 words correct per minute. Proceed to Unit 20 with added fluency practice, or provide Extra Practice lessons in Unit 19, and/or provide a Jell-Well Review.
NO PASS	The student scores 3 or more errors on the first pass through the passage and/or reads 33 or fewer words correct per minute. Provide Extra Practice lessons and retest, and/or provide a Jell-Well Review.

SOUNDS

ĕ	Th	r	k	oo	E	ar	wh
i	sh	ee	Wh	a	ĕ	H	ea

VOWEL DISCRIMINATION

set	sat	sit	seat
Mark	Mick	Mack	meek

BEGINNING QUICK SOUNDS

dent	hand	test	dark
hit	tent	Kim	dash

BLENDS AND WORD ENDINGS

Trish	snack	creek	kitten
scoot	wham	drink	scat

TRICKY WORDS

where	into	as	wouldn't
what	to	There	are

• Have students read from a clean copy of the Decoding Diagnosis. Record incorrect responses on another copy.
• Use information from both the Unit 19 Decoding Assessment and the Unit 19 Decoding Diagnosis to identify specific skill deficits.

TRICKY WORD WARM-UP

| Are | who | there | What | A |

ORAL READING FLUENCY PASSAGE

A Rest

★We met at noon.   4

We could hear my kitten cry.   10

Where was that kitten?   14

The sad kitten was in the tree.   21

Why was she there?   25

What could she do?   29

She could rest.   32

ORAL READING FLUENCY	Start timing at the ★ Mark errors. Make a single slash in the text (/) at 60 seconds. Have student complete passage. If the student completes the passage in less than 60 seconds, have the student go back to the ★ and continue reading. Make a double slash (//) in the text at 60 seconds.
WCPM	Determine words correct per minute by subtracting errors from words read in 60 seconds.
STRONG PASS	The student scores no more than 2 errors on the first pass through the passage and reads a minimum of 46 or more words correct per minute. Proceed to Unit 21.
WEAK PASS	The student scores no more than 2 errors on the first pass through the passage and reads 36 to 45 words correct per minute. Proceed to Unit 21 with added fluency practice, or provide Extra Practice lessons in Unit 20, and/or provide a Jell-Well Review.
NO PASS	The student scores 3 or more errors on the first pass through the passage and/or reads 35 or fewer words correct per minute. Provide Extra Practice lessons and retest, and/or provide a Jell-Well Review.

TRICKY WORD WARM-UP

| one | who | are | wanted | where |

ORAL READING FLUENCY PASSAGE

The Little Tan Kitten

★A little tan kitten went into the den.   8

His dad said, "Sit still. There is a rat."   17

The kitten said, "Look! I see two rats!"   25

The rats said, "We hear two cats."   32

Then the rats ran and hid.   38

ORAL READING FLUENCY	Start timing at the ★. Mark errors. Make a single slash in the text (/) at 60 seconds. Have student complete passage. If the student completes the passage in less than 60 seconds, have the student go back to the ★ and continue reading. Make a double slash (//) in the text at 60 seconds.
WCPM	Determine words correct per minute by subtracting errors from words read in 60 seconds.
STRONG PASS	The student scores no more than 2 errors on the first pass through the passage and reads a minimum of 49 or more words correct per minute. Proceed to Unit 22.
WEAK PASS	The student scores no more than 2 errors on the first pass through the passage and reads 38 to 48 words correct per minute. Proceed to Unit 22 with added fluency practice, or provide Extra Practice lessons in Unit 21, and/or provide a Jell-Well Review.
NO PASS	The student scores 3 or more errors on the first pass through the passage and/or reads 37 or fewer words correct per minute. Provide Extra Practice lessons and retest, and/or provide a Jell-Well Review.

TRICKY WORD WARM-UP

two	his	should	wanted	there

ORAL READING FLUENCY PASSAGE

A Nest

★ What do we see? We see a nest.　　　8

Where is that nest? It's in the tree.　　　16

Where is that tree? It is on a rock.　　　25

Where is that rock? It's not on land.　　　33

It is in the sea.　　　38

ORAL READING FLUENCY	Start timing at the ★. Mark errors. Make a single slash in the text (/) at 60 seconds. Have student complete passage. If the student completes the passage in less than 60 seconds, have the student go back to the ★ and continue reading. Make a double slash (//) in the text at 60 seconds.
WCPM	Determine words correct per minute by subtracting errors from words read in 60 seconds.
STRONG PASS	The student scores no more than 2 errors on the first pass through the passage and reads a minimum of 52 or more words correct per minute. Proceed to Unit 23.
WEAK PASS	The student scores no more than 2 errors on the first pass through the passage and reads 41 to 51 words correct per minute. Proceed to Unit 23 with added fluency practice, or provide Extra Practice lessons in Unit 22, and/or provide a Jell-Well Review.
NO PASS	The student scores 3 or more errors on the first pass through the passage and/or reads 40 or fewer words correct per minute. Provide Extra Practice lessons and retest, and/or provide a Jell-Well Review.

CRITICAL ASSESSMENT

TRICKY WORD WARM-UP

two	listens	because	Look	one

ORAL READING FLUENCY PASSAGE

The Cat

★Little Bill started to cry because   6

he lost his cat. "Where can he be?   14

Will he be back soon?" Then there   21

was a small cry. The cat was by the   30

clock. The cat sat near Bill's best bat.   38

All was well.   41

ORAL READING FLUENCY	Start timing at the ★. Mark errors. Make a single slash in the text (/) at 60 seconds. Have student complete passage. If the student completes the passage in less than 60 seconds, have the student go back to the ★ and continue reading. Make a double slash (//) in the text at 60 seconds.
WCPM	Determine words correct per minute by subtracting errors from words read in 60 seconds.
STRONG PASS	The student scores no more than 2 errors on the first pass through the passage and reads a minimum of 55 or more words correct per minute. Proceed to Unit 24.
WEAK PASS	The student scores no more than 2 errors on the first pass through the passage and reads 44 to 54 words correct per minute. Proceed to Unit 24 with added fluency practice, or provide Extra Practice lessons in Unit 23, and/or provide a Jell-Well Review.
NO PASS	The student scores 3 or more errors on the first pass through the passage and/or reads 43 or fewer words correct per minute. Provide Extra Practice lessons and retest, and/or provide a Jell-Well Review.

SOUNDS

b	ě	R	oo	k	l	-y	o
ea	L	ar	i	B	th	wh	b

VOWEL DISCRIMINATION

Ben	ban	bun	bean
clock	click	clack	cluck

BEGINNING QUICK SOUNDS

barn	call	Ted	kit
duck	hoot	boot	den

BLENDS AND WORD ENDINGS

landed	stream	small	clean
wishes	black	needle	skidded

TRICKY WORDS

about	look	because	two
Who	listens	one	are

- Have students read from a clean copy of the Decoding Diagnosis. Record incorrect responses on another copy.
- Use information from both the Unit 23 Oral Reading Fluency Assessment and the Unit 23 Decoding Diagnosis to identify specific skill deficits.

TRICKY WORD WARM-UP

no	two	because	one	about

ORAL READING FLUENCY PASSAGE

Big Bad Bill

★We got a small kitten that we   7

wanted to call Big Bad Bill. This   14

strong kitten was not shy. He would go   22

where we went. He would get on my   30

bed. He would get into Mom's room.   37

Mom would be so mad.   42

ORAL READING FLUENCY	Start timing at the ★. Mark errors. Make a single slash in the text (/) at 60 seconds. Have student complete passage. If the student completes the passage in less than 60 seconds, have the student go back to the ★ and continue reading. Make a double slash (//) in the text at 60 seconds.
WCPM	Determine words correct per minute by subtracting errors from words read in 60 seconds.
STRONG PASS	The student scores no more than 2 errors on the first pass through the passage and reads a minimum of 58 or more words correct per minute. Proceed to Unit 25.
WEAK PASS	The student scores no more than 2 errors on the first pass through the passage and reads 46 to 57 words correct per minute. Proceed to Unit 25 with added fluency practice, or provide Extra Practice lessons in Unit 24, and/or provide a Jell-Well Review.
NO PASS	The student scores 3 or more errors on the first pass through the passage and/or reads 45 or fewer words correct per minute. Provide Extra Practice lessons and retest, and/or provide a Jell-Well Review.

TRICKY WORD WARM-UP

work	about	eggs	no	who

ORAL READING FLUENCY PASSAGE

Go, Fly, Go

★There was a big fly in my room. It had   10

long wings. It landed on my fish tank.   18

Fred said, "The fish will eat that fly."   26

So I said, "Get off, fly." The fly was foolish.   36

He fell into the fish tank because he went   45

too fast.   47

ORAL READING FLUENCY	Start timing at the ★ Mark errors. Make a single slash in the text (/) at 60 seconds. Have student complete passage. If the student completes the passage in less than 60 seconds, have the student go back to the ★ and continue reading. Make a double slash (//) in the text at 60 seconds.
WCPM	Determine words correct per minute by subtracting errors from words read in 60 seconds.
STRONG PASS	The student scores no more than 2 errors on the first pass through the passage and reads a minimum of 60 or more words correct per minute. Proceed to Unit 26.
WEAK PASS	The student scores no more than 2 errors on the first pass through the passage and reads 46 to 59 words correct per minute. Proceed to Unit 26 with added fluency practice, or provide Extra Practice lessons in Unit 25, and/or provide a Jell-Well Review.
NO PASS	The student scores 3 or more errors on the first pass through the passage and/or reads 45 or fewer words correct per minute. Provide Extra Practice lessons and retest, and/or provide a Jell-Well Review.

CRITICAL ASSESSMENT

TRICKY WORD WARM-UP

what	legs	shouldn't	friends	two

ORAL READING FLUENCY PASSAGE

Fun in the Sun

★The sun was hot. My friends and I   8

wanted to swim. We asked Dad if he   16

would go with us. Dad said, "I am   24

working until three. Ask Mom about it."   31

Mom said she had to dust, but then   39

she could go. She said, "That will be fun."   48

ORAL READING FLUENCY	Start timing at the ★. Mark errors. Make a single slash in the text (/) at 60 seconds. Have student complete passage. If the student completes the passage in less than 60 seconds, have the student go back to the ★ and continue reading. Make a double slash (//) in the text at 60 seconds.
WCPM	Determine words correct per minute by subtracting errors from words read in 60 seconds.
STRONG PASS	The student scores no more than 2 errors on the first pass through the passage and reads a minimum of 65 or more words correct per minute. Proceed to Unit 27.
PASS	The student scores no more than 2 errors on the first pass through the passage and reads 56 to 64 words correct per minute. Proceed to Unit 27.
WEAK PASS	The student scores no more than 2 errors on the first pass through the passage and reads 48 to 55 words correct per minute. Proceed to Unit 27 with added fluency practice, or provide Extra Practice lessons in Unit 26, and/or provide a Jell-Well Review.
NO PASS	The student scores 3 or more errors on the first pass through the passage and/or reads 47 or fewer words correct per minute. Provide Extra Practice lessons and retest, and/or provide a Jell-Well Review.

Note: The "smile" over the e is no longer included. If the student says /ē/, ask if he or she knows another sound.

SOUNDS

u	F	b	i	l	oo	G	ea
s	a	k	U	r	h	f	e

VOWEL DISCRIMINATION

must	fast	mist	lost	nest
fly	flea	shy	she	shed

BEGINNING QUICK SOUNDS

back	dust	hug	goof	Cass
get	tick	heat	dog	beet

BLENDS AND WORD ENDINGS

thing	bleed	little	asked	shark
hunted	song	scrub	cream	resting

TRICKY WORDS

there	from	worked	about	wanted
isn't	eggs	two	Was	A

- Have students read from a clean copy of the Decoding Diagnosis. Record incorrect responses on another copy.
- Use information from both the Unit 26 Decoding Assessment and the Unit 26 Decoding Diagnosis to identify specific skill deficits.

TRICKY WORD WARM-UP

| because | worked | mother | from | brother |

ORAL READING FLUENCY PASSAGE

Best Friends

★Tom and Martin were best friends.   6

Tom said, "I am going to school to hit balls."   16

Martin asked, "Can I go?"   21

Tom said, "That would be great fun!   28

We can hit balls into the sky and under the   38

stands."   39

The two friends went to school and hit balls   48

until it got dark.   52

ORAL READING FLUENCY	Start timing at the ★. Mark errors. Make a single slash in the text (/) at 60 seconds. Have student complete passage. If the student completes the passage in less than 60 seconds, have the student go back to the ★ and continue reading. Make a double slash (//) in the text at 60 seconds.
WCPM	Determine words correct per minute by subtracting errors from words read in 60 seconds.
STRONG PASS	The student scores no more than 2 errors on the first pass through the passage and reads a minimum of 68 or more words correct per minute. Proceed to Unit 28.
PASS	The student scores no more than 2 errors on the first pass through the passage and reads 58 to 67 words correct per minute. Proceed to Unit 28.
WEAK PASS	The student scores no more than 2 errors on the first pass through the passage and reads 49 to 57 words correct per minute. Proceed to Unit 28 with added fluency practice, or provide Extra Practice lessons in Unit 27, and/or provide a Jell-Well Review.
NO PASS	The student scores 3 or more errors on the first pass through the passage and/or reads 48 or fewer words correct per minute. Provide Extra Practice lessons and retest, and/or provide a Jell-Well Review.

    Blackline Master   151

CRITICAL ASSESSMENT

TRICKY WORD WARM-UP

your	father	America	friend	school

ORAL READING FLUENCY PASSAGE

Beth's Lost Yarn

★Beth began to yell. Grandfather asked, "What's　　　　7

the matter?"　　　　9

Beth said, "I lost my yarn!"　　　　15

Grandfather asked, "Where were you?"　　　　20

Beth said, "I went across the street."　　　　27

"Do you remember where you went from there?"　　　　35

said Grandfather.　　　　37

"Yes!" said Beth. "I sat under the tree in Ann's yard."　　　　48

Grandfather said, "We must go back there."　　　　55

ORAL READING FLUENCY	Start timing at the ★ Mark errors. Make a single slash in the text (/) at 60 seconds. Have student complete passage. If the student completes the passage in less than 60 seconds, have the student go back to the ★ and continue reading. Make a double slash (//) in the text at 60 seconds.
WCPM	Determine words correct per minute by subtracting errors from words read in 60 seconds.
STRONG PASS	The student scores no more than 2 errors on the first pass through the passage and reads a minimum of 71 or more words correct per minute. Proceed to Unit 29.
PASS	The student scores no more than 2 errors on the first pass through the passage and reads 60 to 70 words correct per minute. Proceed to Unit 29.
WEAK PASS	The student scores no more than 2 errors on the first pass through the passage and reads 50 to 59 words correct per minute. Proceed to Unit 29 with added fluency practice, or provide Extra Practice lessons in Unit 28, and/or provide a Jell-Well Review.
NO PASS	The student scores 3 or more errors on the first pass through the passage and/or reads 49 or fewer words correct per minute. Provide Extra Practice lessons and retest, and/or provide a Jell-Well Review.

SOUNDS

f	Y	er	g	oo	t	y	a
b	U	y	sh	d	ee	w	R

VOWEL DISCRIMINATION

list	lost	last	let	loot
Barn	bun	bin	band	bend

BEGINNING QUICK SOUNDS

gets	test	cut	bark	hill
dock	hum	kiss	goo	bat

BLENDS AND WORD ENDINGS

basket	stun	desk	grumble	eating
crying	rested	across	teeth	twister

TRICKY WORDS

you	there	brother	do	aren't
were	from	hasn't	what	who

- Have students read from a clean copy of the Decoding Diagnosis. Record incorrect responses on another copy.
- Use information from both the Unit 28 Decoding Assessment and the Unit 28 Decoding Diagnosis to identify specific skill deficits.

TRICKY WORD WARM-UP

ago	worked	they	your	story

ORAL READING FLUENCY PASSAGE

The Park

★Grandmother asked me to go to the park. 8

She said, "It's a long way to the park, so I will 20

stop by to get you at noon." 27

We had things to play with and things to eat. 37

What a fun day together! 42

Grandmother said, "Let's get going." 47

I said, "I do not want to go, but I understand that 59

we must." 61

ORAL READING FLUENCY	Start timing at the ★ Mark errors. Make a single slash in the text (/) at 60 seconds. Have student complete passage. If the student completes the passage in less than 60 seconds, have the student go back to the ★ and continue reading. Make a double slash (//) in the text at 60 seconds.
WCPM	Determine words correct per minute by subtracting errors from words read in 60 seconds.
STRONG PASS	The student scores no more than 2 errors on the first pass through the passage and reads a minimum of 74 or more words correct per minute. Proceed to Unit 30.
PASS	The student scores no more than 2 errors on the first pass through the passage and reads 62 to 73 words correct per minute. Proceed to Unit 30.
WEAK PASS	The student scores no more than 2 errors on the first pass through the passage and reads 51 to 61 words correct per minute. Proceed to Unit 30 with added fluency practice, or provide Extra Practice lessons in Unit 29, and/or provide a Jell-Well Review.
NO PASS	The student scores 3 or more errors on the first pass through the passage and/or reads 50 or fewer words correct per minute. Provide Extra Practice lessons and retest, and/or provide a Jell-Well Review.

TRICKY WORD WARM-UP

They	of	people	earth	were

ORAL READING FLUENCY PASSAGE

The Farm

★ I live on a small farm by a river. The animals   11
on the farm give us lots of food. We get eggs   22
from the hens. We get meat from the pigs.   31

　　All of the people living on the farm have work   41
to do. I have to feed the animals. It can be   52
hard work. But, I do not want to ever go away   63
from my farm.   66

ORAL READING FLUENCY	Start timing at the ★ Mark errors. Make a single slash in the text (/) at 60 seconds. Have student complete passage. If the student completes the passage in less than 60 seconds, have the student go back to the ★ and continue reading. Make a double slash (//) in the text at 60 seconds.
WCPM	Determine words correct per minute by subtracting errors from words read in 60 seconds.
STRONG PASS	The student scores no more than 2 errors on the first pass through the passage and reads a minimum of 77 or more words correct per minute. Proceed to Unit 31.
PASS	The student scores no more than 2 errors on the first pass through the passage and reads 64 to 76 words correct per minute. Proceed to Unit 31.
WEAK PASS	The student scores no more than 2 errors on the first pass through the passage and reads 52 to 63 words correct per minute. Proceed to Unit 31 with added fluency practice, or provide Extra Practice lessons in Unit 30, and/or provide a Jell-Well Review.
NO PASS	The student scores 3 or more errors on the first pass through the passage and/or reads 51 or fewer words correct per minute. Provide Extra Practice lessons and retest, and/or provide a Jell-Well Review.

SOUNDS

U	p	l	v	f	Y	b	ar
g	a	d	o	th	e	V	C

VOWEL DISCRIMINATION

why	win	wee	wham	when
spoon	spin	span	spun	spend

BEGINNING QUICK SOUNDS

tan	cut	bead	give	hard
kept	gap	day	tug	pot

BLENDS AND WORD ENDINGS

living	rumble	darken	along	steam
called	melted	crust	erupt	spring

TRICKY WORDS

earth	of	story	people	your
animal	they	want	what	were

- Have students read from a clean copy of the Decoding Diagnosis. Record incorrect responses on another copy.
- Use information from both the Unit 30 Decoding Assessment and the Unit 30 Decoding Diagnosis to identify specific skill deficits.

TRICKY WORD WARM-UP

from	animals	father	of	even

ORAL READING FLUENCY PASSAGE

My Brother

★ My brother bugs me. One day he said, "You have   10
hundreds of ants in your room."   16

I said, "Stop. Do not play tricks. I have never had ants   28
in my room."   31

He said, "You better be quick. Ants are under your bed.   42
Soon they will be in your bed."   49

I said, "Bill, quit that. You always try to trick me."   60

Bill said, "You better go look."   66

ORAL READING FLUENCY	Start timing at the ★ Mark errors. Make a single slash in the text (/) at 60 seconds. Have student complete passage. If the student completes the passage in less than 60 seconds, have the student go back to the ★ and continue reading. Make a double slash (//) in the text at 60 seconds.
WCPM	Determine words correct per minute by subtracting errors from words read in 60 seconds.
STRONG PASS	The student scores no more than 2 errors on the first pass through the passage and reads a minimum of 80 or more words correct per minute. Proceed to Unit 32.
PASS	The student scores no more than 2 errors on the first pass through the passage and reads 66 to 79 words correct per minute. Proceed to Unit 32.
WEAK PASS	The student scores no more than 2 errors on the first pass through the passage and reads 53 to 65 words correct per minute. Proceed to Unit 32 with added fluency practice, or provide Extra Practice lessons in Unit 31, and/or provide a Jell-Well Review.
NO PASS	The student scores 3 or more errors on the first pass through the passage and/or reads 52 or fewer words correct per minute. Provide Extra Practice lessons and retest, and/or provide a Jell-Well Review.

TRICKY WORD WARM-UP

even	they	your	of	done

ORAL READING FLUENCY PASSAGE

My Job

★All the kids in my class do things to help. My   11

job is to clean the desks. When Miss Smith asked   21

who wanted this job, I jumped up as quick as a wink!   33

So she said, "You can have the job."   41

    I come in and scrub the tops of the desks. Some   52

days my job can be hard. This week there was   62

jam stuck on lots of the desks. Yuck!   70

ORAL READING FLUENCY	Start timing at the ★ Mark errors. Make a single slash in the text (/) at 60 seconds. Have student complete passage. If the student completes the passage in less than 60 seconds, have the student go back to the ★ and continue reading. Make a double slash (//) in the text at 60 seconds.
WCPM	Determine words correct per minute by subtracting errors from words read in 60 seconds.
STRONG PASS	The student scores no more than 2 errors on the first pass through the passage and reads a minimum of 83 or more words correct per minute. Proceed to Unit 33.
PASS	The student scores no more than 2 errors on the first pass through the passage and reads 68 to 82 words correct per minute. Proceed to Unit 33.
WEAK PASS	The student scores no more than 2 errors on the first pass through the passage and reads 54 to 67 words correct per minute. Proceed to Unit 33 with added fluency practice, or provide Extra Practice lessons in Unit 32, and/or provide a Jell-Well Review.
NO PASS	The student scores 3 or more errors on the first pass through the passage and/or reads 53 or fewer words correct per minute. Provide Extra Practice lessons and retest, and/or provide a Jell-Well Review.

TRICKY WORD WARM-UP

because	some	earth	friend	come

ORAL READING FLUENCY PASSAGE

My Sister

★My sister and I get along together. One day I asked   11

her if she would fix my ball for me. She said, "Yes, but   24

you must do something for me."   30

    I asked her what she wanted done. She said,   39

"I will fix your ball and you can clean my room. It should   52

be quick."   54

    My sister fixed my ball, and I cleaned her room. Then   65

we went to the park to play. We have fun.   75

ORAL READING FLUENCY	Start timing at the ★. Mark errors. Make a single slash in the text (/) at 60 seconds. Have student complete passage. If the student completes the passage in less than 60 seconds, have the student go back to the ★ and continue reading. Make a double slash (//) in the text at 60 seconds.
WCPM	Determine words correct per minute by subtracting errors from words read in 60 seconds.
STRONG PASS	The student scores no more than 2 errors on the first pass through the passage and reads a minimum of 86 or more words correct per minute. Proceed to Unit 34.
PASS	The student scores no more than 2 errors on the first pass through the passage and reads 70 to 85 words correct per minute. Proceed to Unit 34.
WEAK PASS	The student scores no more than 2 errors on the first pass through the passage and reads 55 to 69 words correct per minute. Proceed to Unit 34 with added fluency practice, or provide Extra Practice lessons in Unit 33, and/or provide a Jell-Well Review.
NO PASS	The student scores 3 or more errors on the first pass through the passage and/or reads 54 or fewer words correct per minute. Provide Extra Practice lessons and retest, and/or provide a Jell-Well Review.

TRICKY WORD WARM-UP

school	gone	yourself	from	what

ORAL READING FLUENCY PASSAGE

The Zoo

★ There are lots of different animals at the zoo.   9

You can see zebras, foxes, and tame kangaroos.   17

You may see an anteater hanging in a tree. You may   28

even get to visit the "King of the Jungle."   37

    The fun begins as soon as they let you in the   48

gate. You will not want to quit until it gets late.   59

By then you will be glad that you came. Do you want to   72

ask your mom if you can come back some other day?   83

ORAL READING FLUENCY	Start timing at the ★ Mark errors. Make a single slash in the text (/) at 60 seconds. Have student complete passage. If the student completes the passage in less than 60 seconds, have the student go back to the ★ and continue reading. Make a double slash (//) in the text at 60 seconds.
WCPM	Determine words correct per minute by subtracting errors from words read in 60 seconds.
STRONG PASS	The student scores no more than 2 errors on the first pass through the passage and reads a minimum of 89 or more words correct per minute. Proceed to Unit 35.
PASS	The student scores no more than 2 errors on the first pass through the passage and reads 72 to 88 words correct per minute. Proceed to Unit 35.
WEAK PASS	The student scores no more than 2 errors on the first pass through the passage and reads 56 to 71 words correct per minute. Proceed to Unit 35 with added fluency practice, or provide Extra Practice lessons in Unit 34, and/or provide a Jell-Well Review.
NO PASS	The student scores 3 or more errors on the first pass through the passage and/or reads 55 or fewer words correct per minute. Provide Extra Practice lessons and retest, and/or provide a Jell-Well Review.

SOUNDS

y	ar	Z	h	ea	r	v	N
u	t	l	o	qu	D	f	l

VOWEL DISCRIMINATION

hut	hit	hot	hat	hoot
rim	ram	room	rum	ream

BEGINNING QUICK SOUNDS

pest	hard	jazz	gate	teen
Jill	box	cup	base	dash

BLENDS AND WORD ENDINGS

hanging	forever	cleaning	sniffed	hate
spots	quit	startle	maybe	zipper

TRICKY WORDS

story	gone	mother	legs	where
friends	were	done	they	worked

• Have students read from a clean copy of the Decoding Diagnosis. Record incorrect responses on another copy.
• Use information from both the Unit 34 Decoding Assessment and the Unit 34 Decoding Diagnosis to identify specific skill deficits.

TRICKY WORD WARM-UP

very	water	fiction	any	their

ORAL READING FLUENCY PASSAGE

Zack

★ I made many friends at camp last year. My   9

best friend was Zack. We were lucky to be there   19

together. We had a lot of fun.   26

In the morning, we would do art work. In   35

the afternoon we would go for a swim in the lake.   46

We jumped into the cold water. When we went   55

to bed, one of us would make up a funny story to   67

tell the other. We will be friends forever.   75

When I think about going back to camp next   84

year, I feel very happy.   89

ORAL READING FLUENCY	Start timing at the ★ Mark errors. Make a single slash in the text (/) at 60 seconds. Have student complete passage. If the student completes the passage in less than 60 seconds, have the student go back to the ★ and continue reading. Make a double slash (//) in the text at 60 seconds.
WCPM	Determine words correct per minute by subtracting errors from words read in 60 seconds.
STRONG PASS	The student scores no more than 2 errors on the first pass through the passage and reads a minimum of 92 or more words correct per minute. Proceed to Unit 36.
PASS	The student scores no more than 2 errors on the first pass through the passage and reads 74 to 91 words correct per minute. Proceed to Unit 36.
WEAK PASS	The student scores no more than 2 errors on the first pass through the passage and reads 57 to 73 words correct per minute. Proceed to Unit 36 with added fluency practice, or provide Extra Practice lessons in Unit 35, and/or provide a Jell-Well Review.
NO PASS	The student scores 3 or more errors on the first pass through the passage and/or reads 56 or fewer words correct per minute. Provide Extra Practice lessons and retest, and/or provide a Jell-Well Review.

TRICKY WORD WARM-UP

their	any	everywhere	what	laughed

ORAL READING FLUENCY PASSAGE

My Missing Cat

★I keep my cat indoors. However, last week he got out.   11

He ran away for two days. We went all around town shouting   23

his name. He couldn't be found.   29

    So we ran an ad for the cat. The next day, a man came   43

to the door with my cat. That funny cat didn't even make a   56

sound. He just jumped down from the man's arms and quickly   67

ran to me. I was very happy to have my cat back. He had a   82

big snack, and then he went to sleep on my lap.   93

ORAL READING FLUENCY	Start timing at the ★ Mark errors. Make a single slash in the text (/) at 60 seconds. Have student complete passage. If the student completes the passage in less than 60 seconds, have the student go back to the ★ and continue reading. Make a double slash (//) in the text at 60 seconds.
WCPM	Determine words correct per minute by subtracting errors from words read in 60 seconds.
STRONG PASS	The student scores no more than 2 errors on the first pass through the passage and reads a minimum of 95 or more words correct per minute. Proceed to Unit 37.
PASS	The student scores no more than 2 errors on the first pass through the passage and reads 76 to 94 words correct per minute. Proceed to Unit 37.
WEAK PASS	The student scores no more than 2 errors on the first pass through the passage and reads 58 to 75 words correct per minute. Proceed to Unit 37 with added fluency practice, or provide Extra Practice lessons in Unit 36, and/or provide a Jell-Well Review.
NO PASS	The student scores 3 or more errors on the first pass through the passage and/or reads 57 or fewer words correct per minute. Provide Extra Practice lessons and retest, and/or provide a Jell-Well Review.

SOUNDS

S	ea	ou	o	x	n	t	qu
i	z	c	r	ow	oo	K	ar

VOWEL DISCRIMINATION

bay	bar	bee	boo	by
eat	at	it	art	out

BEGINNING QUICK SOUNDS

town	jar	dog	pound	base
gun	bead	win	kiss	howl

BLENDS AND WORD ENDINGS

fact	raining	drops	sky	waves
ground	happy	little	darken	example

TRICKY WORDS

laughed	rain	father	any	your
their	very	learned	come	they

• Have students read from a clean copy of the Decoding Diagnosis. Record incorrect responses on another copy.
• Use information from both the Unit 36 Decoding Assessment and the Unit 36 Decoding Diagnosis to identify specific skill deficits.

TRICKY WORD WARM-UP

many	laugh	pretty	head	their

ORAL READING FLUENCY PASSAGE

Chuck the Frog

★ Once upon a time, there was a little green frog named Chuck.   12

He was such a funny frog that he could make everyone laugh   24

out loud.   26

Each day, Chuck would tell the other frogs a funny story.   37

They would laugh so hard that they would fall down. At last,   49

two of the frogs said, "Chuck, we really like you. But we can't   62

take this laughing anymore."   66

Chuck was speechless. He stopped being funny.   73

Soon, the other frogs were very sad. They said, "Chuck, we   84

need a funny story."   88

Chuck said, "I have just the story for you."   97

ORAL READING FLUENCY	Start timing at the ★. Mark errors. Make a single slash in the text (/) at 60 seconds. Have student complete passage. If the student completes the passage in less than 60 seconds, have the student go back to the ★ and continue reading. Make a double slash (//) in the text at 60 seconds.
WCPM	Determine words correct per minute by subtracting errors from words read in 60 seconds.
STRONG PASS	The student scores no more than 2 errors on the first pass through the passage and reads a minimum of 98 or more words correct per minute. Proceed to Unit 38.
PASS	The student scores no more than 2 errors on the first pass through the passage and reads 78 to 97 words correct per minute. Proceed to Unit 38.
WEAK PASS	The student scores no more than 2 errors on the first pass through the passage and reads 59 to 77 words correct per minute. Proceed to Unit 38 with added fluency practice, or provide Extra Practice lessons in Unit 37, and/or provide a Jell-Well Review.
NO PASS	The student scores 3 or more errors on the first pass through the passage and/or reads 58 or fewer words correct per minute. Provide Extra Practice lessons and retest, and/or provide a Jell-Well Review.

CRITICAL ASSESSMENT

TRICKY WORD WARM-UP

does	only	water	boy	gone

ORAL READING FLUENCY PASSAGE

Take Flight Little Bird

★Chester was a little bird who did not want to fly.   11
His mother said, "Take flight, Chester. You might like it. Look at   23
your brother and sisters. They are having such fun flying high in   35
the sky."   37

Chester said, "It doesn't sound like fun to me."   46

Then one day, Chester's mother told him, "It's getting cold. We   57
must go south for the winter."   63

Chester said, "Not me. I'm staying put."   70

Soon the other birds left. When night fell, Chester was all alone.   82
Suddenly Chester shouted, "Wait for me!"   88

Chester's mother was waiting nearby. She smiled and said,   97
"That's my boy!"   100

ORAL READING FLUENCY	Start timing at the ★ Mark errors. Make a single slash in the text (/) at 60 seconds. Have student complete passage. If the student completes the passage in less than 60 seconds, have the student go back to the ★ and continue reading. Make a double slash (//) in the text at 60 seconds.
WCPM	Determine words correct per minute by subtracting errors from words read in 60 seconds.
STRONG PASS	The student scores no more than 2 errors on the first pass through the passage and reads a minimum of 100 or more words correct per minute. Place the student in *Read Well Plus* or assess for placement in a basal reading program.
PASS	The student scores no more than 2 errors on the first pass through the passage and reads 80 to 99 words correct per minute. Place the student in *Read Well Plus*.
WEAK PASS	The student scores no more than 2 errors on the first pass through the passage and reads 60 to 79 words correct per minute. Place the student in *Read Well Plus*. Provide added fluency practice.
NO PASS	The student scores 3 or more errors on the first pass through the passage and/or reads 59 or fewer words correct per minute. Provide Extra Practice lessons and retest, and/or provide a Jell-Well Review.

SOUNDS

ou	P	ch	ay	j	h	ow	igh
b	qu	Y	o	v	e	d	er

VOWEL DISCRIMINATION

tap	tip	tape	top	tarp
him	harm	hem	hum	high

BEGINNING QUICK SOUNDS

best	pout	jump	girl	chick
cold	drip	her	Tom	call

BLENDS AND WORD ENDINGS

Now	chicken	gather	such	laying
market	brain	clucked	fifteen	inside

TRICKY WORDS

pretty	learn	once	head	water
only	many	their	earth	done

- Have students read from a clean copy of the Decoding Diagnosis. Record incorrect responses on another copy.
- Use information from both the Unit 38 Oral Reading Fluency Assessment and the Unit 38 Decoding Diagnosis to identify specific skill deficits.

STUDENT ASSESSMENT RECORD

Name _____ Teacher _____

IMPORTANT: Follow the scoring and recording procedures shown on pages 64 (Units A–15) and 73 (Units 16–38). For each unit, circle the appropriate pass level: SP (Strong Pass), P (Pass), WP (Weak Pass), or NP (No Pass).

UNIT A	ASSESSMENT ITEMS	SCORE/COMMENTS
Subtest A	I ✂ I ▱ I	Goal 5/5 _____/5 The student is able to track. Yes __ No__
Subtest B	I·I·I III	Goal 2/2 _____/2
Subtest C	I 🧃 ✂ 🦁	Goal 4/4 _____/4
Subtest D	**Who is the story about?** The story is about Olivia.	Goal 1/1 _____/1
Assessment Date(s):		Goals Met _____/4 Subtests **P** (all subtests; proceed to Unit B) **NP** (Provide additional practice and seek consultation.)

UNIT B	ASSESSMENT ITEMS	SCORE/COMMENTS
Subtest A	m 👦 I 🐕 m	Goal 5/5 _____/5 The student is able to track. Yes __ No__
Subtest B	m·m·m mmm I·m I'm	Goal 4/4 _____/4
Subtest C	👦 🦁 I 👧	Goal 4/4 _____/4
Subtest D	**Who is the story about?** The story is about Roberto.	Goal 1/1 _____/1
Assessment Date(s):		Goals Met _____/4 Subtests **P** (all subtests; proceed to Unit 1) **NP** (Provide additional practice and seek consultation.)

STUDENT ASSESSMENT RECORD

Name _____

UNIT I	ASSESSMENT ITEMS	SCORE/COMMENTS
Subtest A	s I I S	Goal 4/4 ____/4 The student is able to track. Yes __ No__
Subtest B	s·s·s sss I·I·I III	Goal 4/4 ____/4
Subtest C	I s S I	Goal 4/4 ____/4
Subtest D	Who is the story about? The story is about Snake. What is she doing? Snake is visiting in her new skin . . .	Goal 2/2 ____/2
Assessment Date(s):		Goals Met ____/4 Subtests P (all subtests) NP

UNIT 2	ASSESSMENT ITEMS	SCORE/COMMENTS
Subtest A	ee s e S	Goal 4/4 ____/4
Subtest B	e·e·e eee s·ee see	Goal 4/4 ____/4
Subtest C	I	Goal I/I ____/I
Subtest D	I see.	Goal 2/2 ____/2
Assessment Date(s):		Goals Met ____/4 Subtests P (all subtests) NP

Name _____

UNIT 3	ASSESSMENT ITEMS	SCORE/COMMENTS
Subtest A	m S e M ee s	Goal 5/6 ____/6
Subtest B	m·m·m mmm m·e me	Goal 4/4 ____/4
Subtest C	I I'm	Goal 2/2 ____/2
Subtest D	I see me.	Goal 3/3 ____/3
Assessment Date(s):		Goals Met ____/4 Subtests P (all subtests) NP

UNIT 4	ASSESSMENT ITEMS	SCORE/COMMENTS
Subtest A	a M e s m A	Goal 5/6 ____/6
Subtest B	a·m am m·e me	Goal 3/4 ____/4
Subtest C	I'm I	Goal 2/2 ____/2
Subtest D	See me. I am Sam.	Goal 5/5 ____/5
Assessment Date(s):		Goals Met ____/4 Subtests P (all subtests) NP

STUDENT ASSESSMENT RECORD

Name _____

UNIT 5	ASSESSMENT ITEMS	SCORE/COMMENTS
Subtest A	D a s ee d M	Goal 5/6 ____/6
Subtest B	a·m am	Goal 2/2 ____/2
Subtest C	dad me add seed	Goal 4/4 ____/4
Subtest D	said I	Goal 2/2 ____/2
Subtest E	I'm mad. Dad said, "I see."	Goal 6/6 ____/6
Assessment Date(s):		Goals Met ____/5 Subtests P (all subtests) NP

UNIT 6	ASSESSMENT ITEMS	SCORE/COMMENTS
Subtest A	A th d e m D	Goal 5/6 ____/6
Subtest B	D·a·d Dad	Goal 2/2 ____/2
Subtest C	am see Dad seeds	Goal 3/4 ____/4
Subtest D	the I'm said	Goal 3/3 ____/3
Subtest E	I said, "See the [cat]. See sad Sam."	Accuracy Goal 7/8 ____/8 words correct ★ Desired Fluency: 20 seconds or less (8/8 in 20 seconds = 24 WCPM) ____ seconds
Assessment Date(s):		Goals Met ____/5 Subtests SP (All subtests with desired fluency) WP (4/5 subtests, and/or fails to attain the desired fluency) NP (Fails two or more subtests)

★ First Timed Reading

Name _____

UNIT 7	ASSESSMENT ITEMS	SCORE/COMMENTS
Subtest A	N a d n ee th	Goal 5/6 ____/6
Subtest B	a·n·d and	Goal 2/2 ____/2
Subtest C	need an seen than	Goal 3/4 ____/4
Subtest D	said I'm the	Goal 3/3 ____/3
Subtest E	I need Dan. "See Nan," said the man.	Accuracy Goal 7/8 ____/8 words correct Desired Fluency: 20 seconds or less (8/8 in 20 seconds = 24 WCPM) ____ seconds
Assessment Date(s):		Goals Met ____/5 Subtests SP (All subtests with desired fluency) WP (4/5 subtests, and/or fails to attain the desired fluency) NP (Fails two or more subtests)

UNIT 8	ASSESSMENT ITEMS	SCORE/COMMENTS
Subtest A	t N e T a th	Goal 5/6 ____/6
Subtest B	th·a·t that	Goal 2/2 ____/2
Subtest C	at seed ants Dad	Goal 3/4 ____/4
Subtest D	I the said	Goal 3/3 ____/3
Subtest E	I sat and sat. Nan meets Sam and me.	Accuracy Goal 8/9 ____/9 words correct Desired Fluency: 20 seconds or less (9/9 in 20 seconds = 27 WCPM) ____ seconds
Assessment Date(s):		Goals Met ____/5 Subtests SP (All subtests with desired fluency) WP (4/5 subtests, and/or fails to attain the desired fluency) NP (Fails two or more subtests)

Name _____

UNIT 9	ASSESSMENT ITEMS	SCORE/COMMENTS
Subtest A	n W M ee t a	Goal 5/6 _____/6
Subtest B	Dan sand that weeds	Goal 3/4 _____/4
Subtest C	was said the	Goal 3/3 _____/3
Subtest D	We see weeds. I see ants and the sad man.	Accuracy Goal 9/10 _____/10 words correct Desired Fluency: 20 seconds or less (10/10 in 20 seconds = 30 WCPM) _____ seconds
Assessment Date(s):		Goals Met _____/4 Subtests SP (All subtests with desired fluency) WP (3/4 subtests, and/or fails to attain the desired fluency) NP (Fails two or more subtests)

UNIT 10	ASSESSMENT ITEMS	SCORE/COMMENTS
Subtest A	w i N a Th e	Goal 5/6 _____/6
Subtest B	it That's did seeds	Goal 3/4 _____/4
Subtest C	I'm was The	Goal 3/3 _____/3
Subtest D	Tim and I sat in the wind. We said, "Did Nan win?"	Accuracy Goal 11/12 _____/12 words correct Desired Fluency: 25 seconds or less (12/12 in 25 seconds = 29 WCPM) _____ seconds
Assessment Date(s):		Goals Met _____/4 Subtests SP (All subtests with desired fluency) WP (3/4 subtests, and/or fails to attain the desired fluency) NP (Fails two or more subtests)

Name _____

UNIT 11	ASSESSMENT ITEMS	SCORE/COMMENTS
Subtest A	h i W ee d H a	Goal 6/7 ____/7
Subtest B	than had we Sam's swim	Goal 4/5 ____/5
Subtest C	as The His was	Goal 3/4 ____/4
Subtest D	He said, "That man is mad." Nat has seeds. Sam's hat was in the sand.	Accuracy Goal 13/15 ____/15 words correct Desired Fluency: 30 seconds or less (15/15 in 30 seconds = 30 WCPM) ____ seconds
Assessment Date(s):		Goals Met ____/4 Subtests SP (All subtests with desired fluency) WP (3/4 subtests, and/or fails to attain the desired fluency) NP (Fails two or more subtests)

UNIT 12	ASSESSMENT ITEMS	SCORE/COMMENTS
Subtest A	N H c e h i C	Goal 6/7 ____/7
Subtest B	hid seen that wind Cass	Goal 4/5 ____/5
Subtest C	hasn't a his isn't	Goal 3/4 ____/4
Subtest D	Tim swims with his dad. We can't see a cat. This can has sand in it.	Accuracy Goal 14/16 ____/16 words correct Desired Fluency: 30 seconds or less (16/16 in 30 seconds = 32 WCPM) ____ seconds
Assessment Date(s):		Goals Met ____/4 Subtests SP (All subtests with desired fluency) WP (3/4 subtests, and/or fails to attain the desired fluency) NP (Fails two or more subtests)

Name _____

UNIT 13	ASSESSMENT ITEMS	SCORE/COMMENTS
Subtest A	r C a d R ea h	Goal 6/7 ____/7
Subtest B	rat He dim can sweet	Goal 4/5 ____/5
Subtest C	is want I'm has	Goal 3/4 ____/4
Subtest D	The deer ran in the mist. Nan meets Sam at the tree. Tad didn't eat with me.	Accuracy Goal 15/17 ____/17 words correct Desired Fluency: 30 seconds or less (17/17 in 30 seconds = 34 WCPM) ____ seconds
Assessment Date(s):		Goals Met ____/4 Subtests SP (All subtests with desired fluency) WP (3/4 subtests, and/or fails to attain the desired fluency) NP (Fails two or more subtests)

UNIT 14	ASSESSMENT ITEMS	SCORE/COMMENTS
Subtest A	Sh w i r e H c	Goal 6/7 ____/7
Subtest B	dash him tree Rats read	Goal 4/5 ____/5
Subtest C	should was said want	Goal 3/4 ____/4
Subtest D	She would swim in the sea. We wish we could meet. The rats should eat a sweet treat.	Accuracy Goal 16/18 ____/18 words correct Desired Fluency: 30 seconds or less (18/18 in 30 seconds = 36 WCPM) ____ seconds
Assessment Date(s):		Goals Met ____/4 Subtests SP (All subtests with desired fluency) WP (3/4 subtests, and/or fails to attain the desired fluency) NP (Fails two or more subtests)

Name _____

UNIT 15	ASSESSMENT ITEMS	SCORE/COMMENTS
Subtest A	k a sh ea i ck r	Goal 6/7 ____/7
Subtest B	creek She can't mean dish	Goal 4/5 ____/5
Subtest C	wants The as said	Goal 3/4 ____/4
Subtest D	Kim and Dee would sit in the sand. Rick couldn't smash that tan hat. Cass said, "I think this trash stinks."	Accuracy Goal 19/21 ____/21 words correct Desired Fluency: 35 seconds or less (21/21 in 35 seconds = 36 WCPM) ____ seconds
Assessment Date(s):		Goals Met ____/4 Subtests SP (All subtests with desired fluency) WP (3/4 subtests, and/or fails to attain the desired fluency) NP (Fails two or more subtests)

UNIT 16	ASSESSMENT ITEMS	SCORE/COMMENTS
Tricky Word Warm-Up	was to his do shouldn't	
Oral Reading Fluency Passage	Did He? ★ Did the raccoon think it was meat? 7 Did the moose crash into Mack? 13 Did the deer swim at noon? 19 Did the moon sink too soon? 25	Accuracy: ____ Passage Errors Desired Fluency: 36+ words correct/minute Fluency: ____ WCPM (____ words read minus ____ errors in one minute)
Assessment Date(s):		SP (No more than 2 errors and 36 or more words correct per minute) WP (No more than 2 errors and 28 to 35 words correct per minute) NP (3 or more errors and/or 27 or fewer words correct per minute)

Name _____

UNIT 17	ASSESSMENT ITEMS	SCORE/COMMENTS
Tricky Word Warm-Up	are couldn't into a wants	

Oral Reading Fluency Passage

Mack's Car

★ Mack sat in his car.   5

The car was in a crash.   11

It wouldn't start.   14

Mack had to think hard.   19

Mack said, "I should ask Dad.   25

He's smart."   27

Accuracy: _____ Passage Errors

Desired Fluency: 39+ words correct/minute

Fluency: _____ WCPM

(_____ words read minus _____ errors in one minute)

Assessment Date(s): _____

SP (No more than 2 errors and 39 or more words correct per minute)
WP (No more than 2 errors and 30 to 38 words correct per minute)
NP (3 or more errors and/or 29 or fewer words correct per minute)

UNIT 18	ASSESSMENT ITEMS	SCORE/COMMENTS
Tricky Word Warm-Up	What Into are do has	

Oral Reading Fluency Passage

Whoosh! Wham!

★ What do I hear?   4

I hear the harsh wind. Whoosh!   10

I hear a tree crash. Wham!   16

What did we do?   20

We hid in the shack.   25

We are smart.   28

Accuracy: _____ Passage Errors

Desired Fluency: 42+ words correct/minute

Fluency: _____ WCPM

(_____ words read minus _____ errors in one minute)

Assessment Date(s): _____

SP (No more than 2 errors and 42 or more words correct per minute)
WP (No more than 2 errors and 32 to 41 words correct per minute)
NP (3 or more errors and/or 31 or fewer words correct per minute)

Name _____

UNIT 19	ASSESSMENT ITEMS	SCORE/COMMENTS
Tricky Word Warm-Up	there what his want are	
Oral Reading Fluency Passage	**Where to Rest?** ★ The red hen went to ask the cat 8 where she should rest. 12 The cat said, "This shed is 18 dark and neat." 21 "Thanks!" said the hen. "That's 26 what I need." 29	Accuracy: _____ Passage Errors Desired Fluency: 44 + words correct/minute Fluency: _____ WCPM (_____ words read minus _____ errors in one minute)

Assessment Date(s):

SP (No more than 2 errors and 44 or more words correct per minute)
WP (No more than 2 errors and 34 to 43 words correct per minute)
NP (3 or more errors and/or 33 or fewer words correct per minute)

UNIT 20	ASSESSMENT ITEMS	SCORE/COMMENTS
Tricky Word Warm-Up	Are who there What A	
Oral Reading Fluency Passage	**A Rest** ★ We met at noon. 4 We could hear my kitten cry. 10 Where was that kitten? 14 The sad kitten was in the tree. 21 Why was she there? 25 What could she do? 29 She could rest. 32	Accuracy: _____ Passage Errors Desired Fluency: 46+ words correct/minute Fluency: _____ WCPM (_____ words read minus _____ errors in one minute)

Assessment Date(s):

SP (No more than 2 errors and 46 or more words correct per minute)
WP (No more than 2 errors and 36 to 45 words correct per minute)
NP (3 or more errors and/or 35 or fewer words correct per minute)

Name _____

UNIT 21	ASSESSMENT ITEMS	SCORE/COMMENTS
Tricky Word Warm-Up	one who are wanted where	
Oral Reading Fluency Passage	The Little Tan Kitten ★ A little tan kitten went into the den.　8 His dad said, "Sit still. There is a rat."　17 The kitten said, "Look! I see two rats!"　25 The rats said, "We hear two cats."　32 Then the rats ran and hid.　38	Accuracy: _____ Passage Errors Desired Fluency: 49+ words correct/minute Fluency: _____ WCPM (_____ words read minus _____ errors in one minute)

Assessment Date(s):

SP (No more than 2 errors and 49 or more words correct per minute)
WP (No more than 2 errors and 38 to 48 words correct per minute)
NP (3 or more errors and/or 37 or fewer words correct per minute)

UNIT 22	ASSESSMENT ITEMS	SCORE/COMMENTS
Tricky Word Warm-Up	two his should wanted there	
Oral Reading Fluency Passage	A Nest ★ What do we see? We see a nest.　8 Where is that nest? It's in the tree.　16 Where is that tree? It is on a rock.　25 Where is that rock? It's not on land.　33 It is in the sea.　38	Accuracy: _____ Passage Errors Desired Fluency: 52+ words correct/minute Fluency: _____ WCPM (_____ words read minus _____ errors in one minute)

Assessment Date(s):

SP (No more than 2 errors and 52 or more words correct per minute)
WP (No more than 2 errors and 41 to 51 words correct per minute)
NP (3 or more errors and/or 40 or fewer words correct per minute)

Name _____

UNIT 23	ASSESSMENT ITEMS	SCORE/COMMENTS
Tricky Word Warm-Up	two listens because Look one	
Oral Reading Fluency Passage	**The Cat** ★ Little Bill started to cry because 6 he lost his cat. "Where can he be? 14 Will he be back soon?" Then there 21 was a small cry. The cat was by the 30 clock. The cat sat near Bill's best bat. 38 All was well. 41	Accuracy: _____ Passage Errors Desired Fluency: 55+ words correct/minute Fluency: _____ WCPM (_____ words read minus _____ errors in one minute)
Assessment Date(s):	SP (No more than 2 errors and 55 or more words correct per minute) WP (No more than 2 errors and 44 to 54 words correct per minute) NP (3 or more errors and/or 43 or fewer words correct per minute)	

UNIT 24	ASSESSMENT ITEMS	SCORE/COMMENTS
Tricky Word Warm-Up	no two because one about	
Oral Reading Fluency Passage	**Big Bad Bill** ★ We got a small kitten that we 7 wanted to call Big Bad Bill. This 14 strong kitten was not shy. He would go 22 where we went. He would get on my 30 bed. He would get into Mom's room. 37 Mom would be so mad. 42	Accuracy: _____ Passage Errors Desired Fluency: 58+ words correct/minute Fluency: _____ WCPM (_____ words read minus _____ errors in one minute)
Assessment Date(s):	SP (No more than 2 errors and 58 or more words correct per minute) WP (No more than 2 errors and 46 to 57 words correct per minute) NP (3 or more errors and/or 45 or fewer words correct per minute)	

Name _____

UNIT 25	ASSESSMENT ITEMS	SCORE/COMMENTS
Tricky Word Warm-Up	work about eggs no who	

Oral Reading Fluency Passage	**Go, Fly, Go**
	
	★There was a big fly in my room. It had 10
	
	long wings. It landed on my fish tank. 18
	
	    Fred said, "The fish will eat that fly." 26
	
	    So I said, "Get off, fly." The fly was foolish. 36
	
	    He fell into the fish tank because he went 45
	
	too fast. 47
		Accuracy: _____ Passage Errors
		
		Desired Fluency: 60+ words correct/minute
		
		Fluency: _____ WCPM
		
		(_____ words read minus _____ errors in one minute)

Assessment Date(s):	**SP** (No more than 2 errors and 60 or more words correct per minute) **WP** (No more than 2 errors and 46 to 59 words correct per minute) **NP** (3 or more errors and/or 45 or fewer words correct per minute)	

UNIT 26	ASSESSMENT ITEMS	SCORE/COMMENTS
Tricky Word Warm-Up	what legs shouldn't friends two	
Oral Reading Fluency Passage	**Fun in the Sun** ★The sun was hot. My friends and I 8 wanted to swim. We asked Dad if he 16 would go with us. Dad said, "I am 24 working until three. Ask Mom about it." 31 Mom said she had to dust, but then 39 she could go. She said, "That will be fun." 48	Accuracy: _____ Passage Errors Desired Fluency: 65+ words correct/minute **Fluency:** _____ WCPM (_____ words read minus _____ errors in one minute)
Assessment Date(s):	**SP** (No more than 2 errors and 65 or more words correct per minute) **P** (No more than 2 errors and 56 to 64 words correct per minute) **WP** (No more than 2 errors and 48 to 55 words correct per minute) **NP** (3 or more errors and/or 47 or fewer words correct per minute)	

Name _____

UNIT 27	ASSESSMENT ITEMS	SCORE/COMMENTS
Tricky Word Warm-Up	because worked mother from brother	
Oral Reading Fluency Passage	**Best Friends** ★ Tom and Martin were best friends.　6 Tom said, "I am going to school to hit balls."　16 Martin asked, "Can I go?"　21 Tom said, "That would be great fun!　28 We can hit balls into the sky and under the　38 stands."　39 The two friends went to school and hit balls　48 until it got dark.　52	**Accuracy:** _____ Passage Errors Desired Fluency: 68+ words correct/minute **Fluency:** _____ WCPM (_____ words read minus _____ errors in one minute)

Assessment Date(s): _____

SP (No more than 2 errors and 68 or more words correct per minute)
P (No more than 2 errors and 58 to 67 words correct per minute)
WP (No more than 2 errors and 49 to 57 words correct per minute)
NP (3 or more errors and/or 48 or fewer words correct per minute)

Name _____

UNIT 28	ASSESSMENT ITEMS	SCORE/COMMENTS
Tricky Word Warm-Up	your father America friend school	

Oral Reading Fluency Passage	**Beth's Lost Yarn**	
	★ Beth began to yell. Grandfather asked, "What's 7	
	the matter?" 9	**Accuracy:** _____
	Beth said, "I lost my yarn!" 15	**Passage Errors**
	Grandfather asked, "Where were you?" 20	Desired Fluency: 71+ words correct/minute
	Beth said, "I went across the street." 27	
	"Do you remember where you went from there?" 35	**Fluency:** _____ WCPM
	said Grandfather. 37	(_____ words read minus _____ errors in one minute)
	"Yes!" said Beth. "I sat under the tree in Ann's yard." 48	
	Grandfather said, "We must go back there." 55	

Assessment Date(s):

SP (No more than 2 errors and 71 or more words correct per minute)
P (No more than 2 errors and 60 to 70 words correct per minute)
WP (No more than 2 errors and 50 to 59 words correct per minute)
NP (3 or more errors and/or 49 or fewer words correct per minute)

Name _____

UNIT 29	ASSESSMENT ITEMS	SCORE/COMMENTS
Tricky Word Warm-Up	ago worked they your story	

Oral Reading Fluency Passage	**The Park**
	
	★Grandmother asked me to go to the park. 8
	
	She said, "It's a long way to the park, so I will 20
	
	stop by to get you at noon." 27
	
	   We had things to play with and things to eat. 37
	
	What a fun day together! 42
	
	   Grandmother said, "Let's get going." 47
	
	   I said, "I do not want to go, but I understand that 59
	
	we must." 61
		Accuracy: _____
		
		Passage Errors
		
		Desired Fluency: 74+ words correct/minute
		
		Fluency: _____ WCPM
		
		(_____ words read minus _____ errors in one minute)

Assessment Date(s): _____

SP (No more than 2 errors and 74 or more words correct per minute)
P (No more than 2 errors and 62 to 73 words correct per minute)
WP (No more than 2 errors and 51 to 61 words correct per minute)
NP (3 or more errors and/or 50 or fewer words correct per minute)

Name _____

UNIT 30	ASSESSMENT ITEMS	SCORE/COMMENTS
Tricky Word Warm-Up	They of people earth were	

Oral Reading Fluency Passage

The Farm

★ I live on a small farm by a river. The animals	11
on the farm give us lots of food. We get eggs	22
from the hens. We get meat from the pigs.	31
All of the people living on the farm have work	41
to do. I have to feed the animals. It can be	52
hard work. But, I do not want to ever go away	63
from my farm.	66

Accuracy: _____

Passage Errors

Desired Fluency: 77+ words correct/minute

Fluency: _____ WCPM

(_____ words read minus _____ errors in one minute)

Assessment Date(s): _____

SP (No more than 2 errors and 77 or more words correct per minute)
P (No more than 2 errors and 64 to 76 words correct per minute)
WP (No more than 2 errors and 52 to 63 words correct per minute)
NP (3 or more errors and/or 51 or fewer words correct per minute)

UNIT 31	ASSESSMENT ITEMS	SCORE/COMMENTS
Tricky Word Warm-Up	from animals father of even	

Oral Reading Fluency Passage

My Brother

★ My brother bugs me. One day he said, "You have	11
hundreds of ants in your room."	16
I said, "Stop. Do not play tricks. I have never had ants	28
in my room."	31
He said, "You better be quick. Ants are under your bed.	42
Soon they will be in your bed."	49
I said, "Bill, quit that. You always try to trick me."	60
Bill said, "You better go look."	66

Accuracy: _____

Passage Errors

Desired Fluency: 80+ words correct/minute

Fluency: _____ WCPM

(_____ words read minus _____ errors in one minute)

Assessment Date(s): _____

SP (No more than 2 errors and 80 or more words correct per minute)
P (No more than 2 errors and 66 to 79 words correct per minute)
WP (No more than 2 errors and 53 to 65 words correct per minute)
NP (3 or more errors and/or 52 or fewer words correct per minute)

Name _____

UNIT 32	ASSESSMENT ITEMS		SCORE/COMMENTS
Tricky Word Warm-Up	even they your of done		
Oral Reading Fluency Passage	**My Job**		**Accuracy:** _____
	★ All the kids in my class do things to help. My	11	**Passage Errors**
	job is to clean the desks. When Miss Smith asked	21	
	who wanted this job, I jumped up as quick as a wink!	33	
	So she said, "You can have the job."	41	Desired Fluency: 83+ words correct/minute
	I come in and scrub the tops of the desks. Some	52	**Fluency:** _____ WCPM
	days my job can be hard. This week there was	62	(_____ words read minus
	jam stuck on lots of the desks. Yuck!	70	_____ errors in one minute)

Assessment Date(s):

SP (No more than 2 errors and 83 or more words correct per minute)
P (No more than 2 errors and 68 to 82 words correct per minute)
WP (No more than 2 errors and 54 to 67 words correct per minute)
NP (3 or more errors and/or 53 or fewer words correct per minute)

UNIT 33	ASSESSMENT ITEMS		SCORE/COMMENTS
Tricky Word Warm-Up	because some earth friend come		
Oral Reading Fluency Passage	**My Sister**		
	★ My sister and I get along together. One day I asked	11	**Accuracy:** _____
	her if she would fix my ball for me. She said, "Yes, but	24	**Passage Errors**
	you must do something for me."	30	
	I asked her what she wanted done. She said,	39	Desired Fluency: 86+ words correct/minute
	"I will fix your ball and you can clean my room. It should	52	
	be quick."	54	**Fluency:** _____ WCPM
	My sister fixed my ball, and I cleaned her room. Then	65	(_____ words read minus
	we went to the park to play. We have fun.	75	_____ errors in one minute)

Assessment Date(s):

SP (No more than 2 errors and 86 or more words correct per minute)
P (No more than 2 errors and 70 to 85 words correct per minute)
WP (No more than 2 errors and 55 to 69 words correct per minute)
NP (3 or more errors and/or 54 or fewer words correct per minute)

Name _____

UNIT 34	ASSESSMENT ITEMS	SCORE/COMMENTS
Tricky Word Warm-Up	school gone yourself from what	
Oral Reading Fluency Passage	**The Zoo** ★ There are lots of different animals at the zoo. 9 You can see zebras, foxes, and tame kangaroos. 17 You may see an anteater hanging in a tree. You may 28 even get to visit the "King of the Jungle." 37 The fun begins as soon as they let you in the 48 gate. You will not want to quit until it gets late. 59 By then you will be glad that you came. Do you want to 72 ask your mom if you can come back some other day? 83	Accuracy: _____ Passage Errors Desired Fluency: 89+ words correct/minute Fluency: _____ WCPM (_____ words read minus _____ errors in one minute)

Assessment Date(s):

SP (No more than 2 errors and 89 or more words correct per minute)
P (No more than 2 errors and 72 to 88 words correct per minute)
WP (No more than 2 errors and 56 to 71 words correct per minute)
NP (3 or more errors and/or 55 or fewer words correct per minute)

Name _____

UNIT 35	ASSESSMENT ITEMS	SCORE/COMMENTS
Tricky Word Warm-Up	very water fiction any their	
Oral Reading Fluency Passage	**Zack**	

	★ I made many friends at camp last year. My	9
	best friend was Zack. We were lucky to be there	19
	together. We had a lot of fun.	26
	In the morning, we would do art work. In	35
	the afternoon we would go for a swim in the lake.	46
	We jumped into the cold water. When we went	55
	to bed, one of us would make up a funny story to	67
	tell the other. We will be friends forever.	75
	When I think about going back to camp next	84
	year, I feel very happy.	89

Accuracy: _____

Passage Errors

Desired Fluency: 92+ words correct/minute

Fluency: _____ WCPM

(_____ words read minus _____ errors in one minute)

Assessment Date(s):

SP (No more than 2 errors and 92 or more words correct per minute)
P (No more than 2 errors and 74 to 91 words correct per minute)
WP (No more than 2 errors and 57 to 73 words correct per minute)
NP (3 or more errors and/or 56 or fewer words correct per minute)

Name _____

UNIT 36	ASSESSMENT ITEMS	SCORE/COMMENTS
Tricky Word Warm-Up	their any everywhere what laughed	
Oral Reading Fluency Passage	**My Missing Cat** ★ I keep my cat indoors. However, last week he got out. 11 He ran away for two days. We went all around town shouting 23 his name. He couldn't be found. 29 So we ran an ad for the cat. The next day, a man came 43 to the door with my cat. That funny cat didn't even make a 56 sound. He just jumped down from the man's arms and quickly 67 ran to me. I was very happy to have my cat back. He had a 82 big snack, and then he went to sleep on my lap. 93	Accuracy: _____ Passage Errors Desired Fluency: 95+ words correct/minute Fluency: _____ WCPM (_____ words read minus _____ errors in one minute)

Assessment Date(s):

SP (No more than 2 errors and 95 or more words correct per minute)
P (No more than 2 errors and 76 to 94 words correct per minute)
WP (No more than 2 errors and 58 to 75 words correct per minute)
NP (3 or more errors and/or 57 or fewer words correct per minute)

Name _____

UNIT 37	ASSESSMENT ITEMS	SCORE/COMMENTS
Tricky Word Warm-Up	many laugh pretty head their	

| Oral Reading Fluency Passage | **Chuck the Frog** | |

★ Once upon a time, there was a little green frog named Chuck. 12

He was such a funny frog that he could make everyone laugh 24

out loud. 26

    Each day, Chuck would tell the other frogs a funny story. 37

They would laugh so hard that they would fall down. At last, 49

two of the frogs said, "Chuck, we really like you. But we can't 62

take this laughing anymore." 66

    Chuck was speechless. He stopped being funny. 73

    Soon, the other frogs were very sad. They said, "Chuck, we 84

need a funny story." 88

    Chuck said, "I have just the story for you." 97

Accuracy: _____
Passage Errors

Desired Fluency: 98+ words correct/minute

Fluency: _____
WCPM

(_____ words read minus _____ errors in one minute)

Assessment Date(s): _____

SP (No more than 2 errors and 98 or more words correct per minute)
P (No more than 2 errors and 78 to 97 words correct per minute)
WP (No more than 2 errors and 59 to 77 words correct per minute)
NP (3 or more errors and/or 58 or fewer words correct per minute)

Name _____

UNIT 38	ASSESSMENT ITEMS	SCORE/COMMENTS
Tricky Word Warm-Up	does only water boy gone	

Oral Reading Fluency Passage	**Take Flight Little Bird**	

★ Chester was a little bird who did not want to fly.   11

His mother said, "Take flight, Chester. You might like it. Look at   23

your brother and sisters. They are having such fun flying high in   35

the sky."   37

Chester said, "It doesn't sound like fun to me."   46

Then one day, Chester's mother told him, "It's getting cold. We   57

must go south for the winter."   63

Chester said, "Not me. I'm staying put."   70

Soon the other birds left. When night fell, Chester was all alone.   82

Suddenly Chester shouted, "Wait for me!"   88

Chester's mother was waiting nearby. She smiled and said,   97

"That's my boy!"   100

Accuracy: _____
Passage Errors

Desired Fluency: 100+ words correct/minute

Fluency: _____
WCPM

(_____ words read – _____ errors/minute)

Assessment Date(s): _____

SP (No more than 2 errors and 100 or more words correct per minute)

P (No more than 2 errors and 80 to 99 words correct per minute)

WP (No more than 2 errors and 60 to 79 words correct per minute)

NP (3 or more errors and/or 59 or fewer words correct per minute)

Directions

1. For each subtest, write the goal in the appropriate column header. (Subtest goals are located at the bottom of each assessment.)
2. For each student and subtest, record the number of correct responses over the number of possible responses (e.g., 4/5). Circle scores of subtests not passed.
3. Using the guide on each Student Assessment Record, determine and record a Pass or a No Pass.
4. For students who do not pass, provide additional practice and retest. Record retest scores to the right of the original scores.

Group Name _____

Student Names	Unit ___ Date ___	Subtest A Tracking, Sounds, and Words Goal ___/___	Subtest B Smooth and Bumpy Blending Goal ___/___	Subtest C Finger Tracking Goal ___/___	Subtest D Comprehension Goal ___/___
	P / NP				
	P / NP				
	P / NP				
	P / NP				
	P / NP				
	P / NP				
	P / NP				
	P / NP				
	P / NP				
	P / NP				
	P / NP				
	P / NP				

Unit ___ Date ___	Subtest A Tracking, Sounds, and Words Goal ___/___	Subtest B Smooth and Bumpy Blending Goal ___/___	Subtest C Finger Tracking Goal ___/___	Subtest D Comprehension Goal ___/___
P / NP				
P / NP				
P / NP				
P / NP				
P / NP				
P / NP				
P / NP				
P / NP				
P / NP				
P / NP				
P / NP				
P / NP				

Directions

1. For each subtest, write the goal in the appropriate column header. (Subtest goals are located at the bottom of each assessment.)
2. For each student and subtest, record the number of correct responses over the number of possible responses (e.g., 4/5). Circle scores of subtests not passed.
3. Using the guide on each Student Assessment Record, determine and record a Pass or a No Pass.
4. For students who do not pass, provide additional practice and retest. Record retest scores to the right of the original scores.

Group Name _____

Student Names	Unit ___ Date ___	Subtest A Sounds Goal __/__	Subtest B Smooth and Bumpy Blending Goal __/__	Subtest C Tricky Words Goal __/__	Subtest D Sentences Goal __/__	Unit ___ Date ___	Subtest A Sounds Goal __/__	Subtest B Smooth and Bumpy Blending Goal __/__	Subtest C Tricky Words Goal __/__	Subtest D Sentences Goal __/__
	P / NP					P / NP				
	P / NP					P / NP				
	P / NP					P / NP				
	P / NP					P / NP				
	P / NP					P / NP				
	P / NP					P / NP				
	P / NP					P / NP				
	P / NP					P / NP				
	P / NP					P / NP				
	P / NP					P / NP				
	P / NP					P / NP				
	P / NP					P / NP				

Directions

1. For each subtest, write the goal in the appropriate column header. (Subtest goals are located at the bottom of each assessment.)
2. For each student and subtest, record the number of correct responses over the number of possible responses (e.g., 4/5). Circle scores of subtests not passed.
3. Using the guide on each Student Assessment Record, determine and record a Pass or a No Pass.
4. For students who do not pass, provide additional practice and retest. Record retest scores to the right of the original scores.

Group Name _____

Student Names	Unit ___ Date ___	Subtest A Sounds Goal __/__	Subtest B Smooth and Bumpy Blending Goal __/__	Subtest C Sounding Out Smoothly Goal __/__	Subtest D Tricky Words Goal __/__	Subtest E Sentences Goal __/__	Unit ___ Date ___	Subtest A Sounds Goal __/__	Subtest B Smooth and Bumpy Blending Goal __/__	Subtest C Sounding Out Smoothly Goal __/__	Subtest D Tricky Words Goal __/__	Subtest E Sentences Goal __/__
	P / NP						P / NP					
	P / NP						P / NP					
	P / NP						P / NP					
	P / NP						P / NP					
	P / NP						P / NP					
	P / NP						P / NP					
	P / NP						P / NP					
	P / NP						P / NP					
	P / NP						P / NP					
	P / NP						P / NP					
	P / NP						P / NP					
	P / NP						P / NP					

Directions

1. For each subtest, write the goal in the appropriate column header. (Subtest goals are located at the bottom of each assessment.)
2. For each student and subtest, record the number of correct responses over the number of possible responses (e.g., 4/5). Circle scores of subtests not passed.
3. For the Sentence Fluency score (ast column), record the number of seconds it takes the student to complete the sentence reading. Circle scores that do not meet the desired fluency goal.
4. Using the guide on each Student Assessment Record, determine and record a Strong Pass, Weak Pass, or a No Pass.
5. For students who do not pass, provide additional practice and retest. Record retest scores to the right of the original scores.

Group Name _____

Student Names	Unit / Date	Subtest A Sounds Goal __/__	Subtest B Smooth and Bumpy Blending Goal __/__	Subtest C Sounding Out Smoothly Goal __/__	Subtest D Tricky Words Goal __/__	Subtest E Sentences Goal __/__	Sentence Fluency Fluency Goal __/__ seconds
	SP / WP / NP						
	SP / WP / NP						
	SP / WP / NP						
	SP / WP / NP						
	SP / WP / NP						
	SP / WP / NP						
	SP / WP / NP						
	SP / WP / NP						
	SP / WP / NP						
	SP / WP / NP						
	SP / WP / NP						

Unit / Date	Subtest A Sounds Goal __/__	Subtest B Smooth and Bumpy Blending Goal __/__	Subtest C Sounding Out Smoothly Goal __/__	Subtest D Tricky Words Goal __/__	Subtest E Sentences Goal __/__	Sentence Fluency Fluency Goal __/__ seconds
SP / WP / NP						
SP / WP / NP						
SP / WP / NP						
SP / WP / NP						
SP / WP / NP						
SP / WP / NP						
SP / WP / NP						
SP / WP / NP						
SP / WP / NP						
SP / WP / NP						
SP / WP / NP						

Directions

1. For each subtest, write the goal in the appropriate column header. (Subtest goals are located at the bottom of each assessment.)
2. For each student and subtest, record the number of correct responses over the number of possible responses (e.g., 4/5). Circle scores of subtests not passed.
3. For the Sentence Fluency score (last column), record the number of seconds it takes the student to complete the sentence reading. Circle scores that do not meet the desired fluency goal.
4. Using the guide on each Student Assessment Record, determine and record a Strong Pass, Weak Pass, or a No Pass.
5. For students who do not pass, provide additional practice and retest. Record retest scores to the right of the original scores.

Group Name _____

Student Names	Unit ____ / Date ____	Subtest A Sounds Goal __/__	Subtest B Sounding Out Smoothly Goal __/__	Subtest C Tricky Words Goal __/__	Subtest D Sentences Goal __/__	Sentence Fluency Desired Fluency Goal __/__
	SP / WP / NP					
	SP / WP / NP					
	SP / WP / NP					
	SP / WP / NP					
	SP / WP / NP					
	SP / WP / NP					
	SP / WP / NP					
	SP / WP / NP					
	SP / WP / NP					
	SP / WP / NP					
	SP / WP / NP					
	SP / WP / NP					

	Unit ____ / Date ____	Subtest A Sounds Goal __/__	Subtest B Sounding Out Smoothly Goal __/__	Subtest C Tricky Words Goal __/__	Subtest D Sentences Goal __/__	Sentence Fluency Desired Fluency Goal __/__
	SP / WP / NP					
	SP / WP / NP					
	SP / WP / NP					
	SP / WP / NP					
	SP / WP / NP					
	SP / WP / NP					
	SP / WP / NP					
	SP / WP / NP					
	SP / WP / NP					
	SP / WP / NP					
	SP / WP / NP					
	SP / WP / NP					

Directions

1. Write the Wcpm for a Strong Pass (SP) in the space provided at the top of the fifth column. (This number is found in the bottom box of the Student Assessment Record and provides an overall goal for instruction.)
2. In the third column, record the number of Tricky Words missed. (List the words at the bottom of the form for reteaching.)
3. For the Passage Accuracy Score (fourth column), record the number of errors the student made the first time he or she read through the whole passage (excluding the title). Do not count any additional errors made if the student begins reading the passage a second time.
4. For the Oral Reading Fluency Score, record the number of words read correctly in one minute minus the number of all errors made during that minute.
5. Using the guide on each Student Assessment Record, determine and record a Strong Pass, Weak Pass, or No Pass.
6. For students who do not pass, provide additional practice and retest. Record retest scores to the right of the original scores.

Group Name _____

Student Names	Unit ___ Date ___	Tricky Word Errors	Passage Accuracy Score Goal 0–2 Errors	Oral Reading Fluency Score SP Goal ___ WCPM	Unit ___ Date ___	Tricky Word Errors	Passage Accuracy Score Goal 0–2 Errors	Oral Reading Fluency Score SP Goal ___ WCPM
	SP / WP / NP				SP / WP / NP			
	SP / WP / NP				SP / WP / NP			
	SP / WP / NP				SP / WP / NP			
	SP / WP / NP				SP / WP / NP			
	SP / WP / NP				SP / WP / NP			
	SP / WP / NP				SP / WP / NP			
	SP / WP / NP				SP / WP / NP			
	SP / WP / NP				SP / WP / NP			
	SP / WP / NP				SP / WP / NP			
	SP / WP / NP				SP / WP / NP			
	SP / WP / NP				SP / WP / NP			

Group Name _____

Directions

1. Write the Wcpm for a Strong Pass (SP) in the space provided at the top of the fifth column. (This number is found in the bottom box of the Student Assessment Record and provides an overall goal for instruction.)

2. In the third column, record the number of Tricky Words missed. (List the words at the top of the fifth column.)

3. For the Passage Accuracy Score (fourth column), record the number of errors the student made the first time he or she read through the whole passage (excluding the title). Do not count any additional errors made if the student begins reading the passage a second time.

4. For the Oral Reading Fluency Score, record the number of words read correctly in one minute minus the number of all errors made during that minute. If the student begins reading the passage a second time, make sure to include those errors.

5. Using the guide on each Student Assessment Record, determine and record a Strong Pass, Pass, Weak Pass, or No Pass.

6. For students who do not pass, provide additional practice and retest. Record retest scores to the right of the original scores.

Student Names	Unit / Date	Tricky Word Errors	Passage Accuracy Score (Goal 0–2 Errors)	Oral Reading Fluency Score (SP Goal ___ WCPM)	Unit / Date	Tricky Word Errors	Passage Accuracy Score (Goal 0–2 Errors)	Oral Reading Fluency Score (SP Goal ___ WCPM)
	SP / P / WP / NP				SP / P / WP / NP			
	SP / P / WP / NP				SP / P / WP / NP			
	SP / P / WP / NP				SP / P / WP / NP			
	SP / P / WP / NP				SP / P / WP / NP			
	SP / P / WP / NP				SP / P / WP / NP			
	SP / P / WP / NP				SP / P / WP / NP			
	SP / P / WP / NP				SP / P / WP / NP			
	SP / P / WP / NP				SP / P / WP / NP			
	SP / P / WP / NP				SP / P / WP / NP			
	SP / P / WP / NP				SP / P / WP / NP			
	SP / P / WP / NP				SP / P / WP / NP			
	SP / WP / NP				SP / WP / NP			